Let's Do This, Folks!

HOME COOKING WITH LORENZO

— DELICIOUS MEALS MADE E-Z —

LORENZO L. BERONILLA

Breakout star of the Epicurious show *4 Levels*

PAGE STREET
PUBLISHING CO.

PAGE STREET
PUBLISHING CO.

Table of Contents

Hello, Folks!

Yes, it's me, Lorenzo, and . . . I WROTE A COOKBOOK!

Before this year, I never would have imagined that writing a book was in the cards for me. There are only two things I do know for sure: one, I love food, and two . . . I really enjoy cooking! Since you're reading this, I imagine these are two things that you and I have in common. So it's official: We're friends now.

Since we're rubbing elbows, I'll let you in on a bit of the history of where I acquired my cooking skills. I remember watching my very first food show as early as 4 years old—it was called My Huge Filipino Family in Our Kitchen. I was the youngest, a little munchkin back then. Whoever was babysitting me at the time would just plop me on the kitchen counter and I'd just . . . watch. I had THE BEST seat in the house, and witnessed hours upon hours of family fun and kitchen cahoots as my entire household rushed around chopping, mixing, steaming, baking, and frying at a frantic, cartoon-like pace. The show was truly Emmy-worthy. And in the end, the results were always the same—AMAZING FOOD.

From the beginning, I wanted to be part of the mix. I didn't want to just watch people cooking, I wanted to BE the guy cooking. So, 15 years ago, I went for it. I practiced my knife skills any chance I got, and I started trying out recipes. I found cooking to be fun and enjoyable, and, surprisingly to some folks, very relaxing. I really loved it because the more time I spent in the kitchen, the more I was bombarded with mouthwatering memories of growing up watching my family cook at home.

As fate would have it, 2 years ago I was given the opportunity to cook on the Epicurious pilot show 4 Levels. The show was, and still is, a big hit, and I became known as "Lorenzo, Home Cook, Level 2 Chef." Who woulda thunk that those crazy family scenes would set me on a culinary path that would impact my life in such a positive way? Hello, I am writing a cookbook!

One of my strengths as a chef is that I've always been willing to attempt any recipe that looks delicious. I've grown confident in my culinary skills through a great deal of trial and error, and it's evident in how and what I cook. I wrote this book hoping that you foodies and chefs in the making will gain the same confidence in your kitchen. There's no need to be afraid to give anything a try. It's just important that you have fun while you're doing it! To help you along the way, look out for my Flip Tips (Filipino tips), which are tidbits of my knowledge and advice about certain aspects of some recipes.

So go ahead—flip through my book, pick any recipe, and soon you'll be cooking amazing food no matter your experience level!

Welcome to
My World of Tapas

I'm THAT guy who would be just fine ordering a bunch of appetizers as my main meal. I mean, who doesn't enjoy snacking on a smorgasbord of food?! I start every meal with an appetizer, so of course I wanted my book to do the same. All of my little food-bite recipes have been categorized as tapas, from my go-to pickable snacks like nachos and dips to my fave party apps like egg rolls, pizza, and crab cakes. And don't miss my double-whammy appetizer from my Filipino roots—tender sweet pork and spiced-up beef tapas.

Welcome to my world of tapas—eat 'em up, folks!

~ QUEKIAM ~
(PORK 'N' SHRIMP EGG ROLLS)

As you know, I'm Filipino—or Flip, as my family refers to us—and Flips . . . make . . . egg rolls. Three of my favorite egg roll recipes of all time are in this book. The first one I want to share is called *Quekiam*. Typically, my family only makes these on special occasions. I've always thought they looked fancy: sliced with precision on the bias (at an angle), perfectly placed on a platter. These egg rolls seem to always wow people at parties, but they're pretty E-Z to put together. If you start off a party with these little guys, folks will surely be impressed, especially if you try them with my Lucky Ducky Sauce (page 152)!

Yields 10 to 12 egg rolls

½ lb (227 g) ground pork

½ lb (227 g) large shrimp, 31–35 count, thawed, peeled, deveined, and each cut into 4 pieces

1 (8-oz [227-g]) can water chestnuts, drained and diced

½ cup (25 g) green onions, chopped

6 large shiitake mushrooms, chopped (fresh is preferred, but dried works too; see Flip Tip)

2 tbsp (30 ml) soy sauce

Pinch of salt and pepper

7 egg yolks, whisked

7 tbsp (56 g) all-purpose flour, divided

1 whole egg

1 package of large spring roll or egg roll wrappers

4 cups (960 ml) veggie oil

In a medium glass bowl, mix the pork, shrimp, water chestnuts, green onions, mushrooms, soy sauce, salt and pepper, egg yolks, and 1 tablespoon (15 g) of the flour. Cover the mixture with plastic wrap, and refrigerate for 10 minutes. This will firm up the filling and marinate the ingredients.

When the 10 minutes are up, scoop the filling mixture into a large sealer bag. Make sure the bag is one that lies flat, with pointy corners—not a gusset bag. Push the filling mixture into one corner of the bag, and release all the air before sealing it. As you might have guessed, we are making a makeshift piping bag! Twist the bag until it's tight and tie off the part with the mixture using a rubber band or twist tie. Cut a 1½-inch (4-cm) opening in one corner of the bag to create a spout. This will create a meat roll 2 inches (5 cm) in diameter.

In a small bowl, whisk the egg and set it aside. This will be the egg wash you use to seal the wrappers.

Divide the remaining flour evenly between two baking sheets. One sheet will be your prep surface and the other is for your wrapped rolls. First, set one wrapper down with a corner facing you, so that it forms a funny-looking diamond—wraps aren't perfectly square, folks! Starting 2 inches (5 cm) from the left corner, squeeze the pork and shrimp mixture onto the wrapper. Try to keep your squeezing consistent, so the mixture comes out in a continuous 2-inch (5-cm) roll, and stop squeezing when you're 2 inches (5 cm) from the right corner. Then take both the left and right corners and fold them over the mixture as if you're wrapping a gift box. Be sure to wrap tightly, otherwise you'll end up with a pan of floating filling and broken wrappers! Take the corner closest to you and fold that tightly over the filling, being careful not to tear the wrapper. Dip your finger into the egg wash and coat the last corner, the one farthest away from you. Fold the coated corner over the filling to seal the wrapper. Place the completed roll, sealed side down, onto your second floured baking sheet. Continue the rolling steps until you have 10 to 12 egg rolls. See page 25 for some photos of this process.

(continued)

QUEKIAM (PORK 'N' SHRIMP EGG ROLLS)
(Continued)

Since your rolls have uncooked, raw ingredients, you MUST do this next step before frying: Poke each roll with a toothpick six to seven times, all around the roll. Make sure you puncture the wrapper through to the meat so the hot oil reaches it.

In a medium-sized pot, heat your oil over low to medium heat—you want the rolls to brown slowly. I like to deep fry only three rolls at a time, so they don't overcrowd the pot—overcrowding cools the oil temperature. Keep an eye on the egg rolls, as the wrapper browns quite easily. Turn them over and over to make sure the entire roll is getting golden brown. Cooking time is short, 3 to 4 minutes.

Grab the rolls out with tongs and place them in a strainer vertically to properly drain excess oil. Let them cool for a few minutes.

Cut the rolls in half on the bias, or at an angle. If you want to be artsy-fartsy, serve your egg rolls arranged on a bed lettuce or ribboned cabbage. Serve them with my sweet 'n' sour Lucky Ducky Sauce (page 152).

YEEHAW! Good for you, you made homemade egg rolls!

FLIP TIP: If you buy the dehydrated mushroom packs, bring them back to life by simmering them in a pot of water for 10 minutes, then straining them using a fine sieve. When the mushrooms are cooled, squeeze the water out of them by hand. Slice up the caps and add them to the mix; discard the tough stems.

~ *TAPA* TENDERS ~
(*TOCINO* PORK / *TAPA* BEEF)

If you ever have a chance to witness or attend a Filipino party, take it! They are truly a unique experience. It's always very loud, there's tons of food, and everyone is constantly telling you to eat. That's where I had my first taste of *tocino*. Talk about delicious!

Tocino and *tapa* (yes, it really is just called tapa), are two types of Filipino tapas, and both are delicious. They are traditionally known as all-day breakfast meals, but I grew up with my family serving them as hors d'oeuvres and appetizers. *Tocino* is made with pork and *tapa* is made with beef, and both are considered cured meats. The recipes are similar, except for two other main ingredients: Pork *tocino* uses rice wine vinegar, and beef *tapa* uses lemon juice, or *calamansi*, a Philippine lime that is the traditional citrus used in this dish.

Serves 12

TOCINO	TAPA
¼ cup (60 ml) soy sauce	¼ cup (60 ml) soy sauce
8 cloves garlic, minced	8 cloves garlic, minced
½ tsp salt	½ tsp salt
¼ tsp freshly ground black pepper	¼ tsp freshly ground black pepper
2 tbsp (30 ml) rice wine vinegar	2 tbsp (30 ml) fresh lemon juice, or *calamansi* juice
1 tbsp (15 g) white sugar	3 tbsp (45 g) white sugar
1 cup (240 ml) soda, like 7 UP, or your choice of fizzy liquid	2 tbsp (28 g) brown sugar
¼ tsp saltpeter, optional	1 cup (240 ml) soda, like 7 UP, or your choice of fizzy liquid
1½ lb (680 g) pork butt (see Flip Tip)	⅛ tsp chili powder, optional
4–5 tbsp (60–75 ml) veggie oil	¼ tsp saltpeter, optional
	1½ lb (680 g) beef sirloin
	4–5 tbsp (60–75 ml) veggie oil

For either tapa recipe, the first step is to combine all of the ingredients except the meat and oil in a large bowl to make the marinade. To make the *tocino*, combine the soy sauce, garlic, salt, pepper, vinegar, white sugar, soda and saltpeter, if using. To make the *tapa*, combine the soy sauce, garlic, salt, pepper, lemon juice, white and brown sugars, soda, and the chili powder, and saltpeter, if using. Set the marinade aside.

Thinly slice the pork and beef into slabs about ⅛ inch (3 mm) thick. Do your best to slice consistently, or next time do what I do—ask the butcher to do it!

The marinade and marinating time are very important to pulling off this delicious dish, but let's go one step further and use a meat mallet to tenderize the sliced meat too. If you don't have a mallet, you can use a rolling pin or a heavy skillet. Place the slabs of meat between two sheets of plastic wrap. Pound the meat for about a minute on each side. This will break up and soften the fibers, making the meat easier to chew.

Fizzy liquid also helps tenderize the meat, and if it contains sugar, it helps to form a coating that will char when cooked. Charring, particularly on the pork *tocino*, is yummy, so we WANT it to turn out this way. Saltpeter is an optional ingredient that also tenderizes and cures meat. Using it will give the meat the traditional reddish color we Flips grew up seeing.

The meat will need to marinate for at least 8 hours, but the longer the better. I usually put it in the fridge overnight. For the best result, put the meat and marinade in a sealer bag. This way the meat will marinate evenly.

(continued)

TAPA TENDERS (*TOCINO* PORK / *TAPA* BEEF)
(Continued)

When the meat is marinated, heat a skillet over medium heat and pour in the veggie oil. It's important to drain as much marinade as possible from the slabs before placing them into the hot oil to avoid splattering. Believe me, I have the scars to attest to the importance of this step! Fry each slab of meat for 4 to 5 minutes per side, or until it's tender and the outside is lightly charred.

A fun alternative is to cook the meat on skewers instead of using a skillet. If you do use wooden skewers, soak them in water for 20 minutes first so they don't burn. Needle the skewer through the meat, keeping the slab whole. Now you have a shish kebab! Either broil or grill until tender and you get that cool charred look.

Serve as an appetizer, or have it like most Filipinos, as a meal with white rice and a fried egg—soooo good!

FLIP TIP: If you can't find pork butt, pork loin is fine too, "butt" we need it fatty. (Relax, pork butt is a cut taken from the upper portion of the shoulder!) For *tapa*, sirloin steak is a must.

⌒ MACHO NACHOS ⌒

The very first time I made this was kind of an accident. I was excited to watch the Olympic Games on TV and stuff myself with nachos, but I forgot the main ingredient—ground beef! So I was faced with the dilemma of either racing to the store and running the risk of missing the opening ceremonies, or just using whatever I had in the fridge. Of course I chose the fridge. I had chicken and lots of beer—no brainer, nachos with chicken it was! That's how Macho Nachos were born. I use a slow cooker for this recipe, not only to tenderize a less expensive cut of meat, but also because long cooking processes bring out all the flavors of the ingredients. It's worth the wait!

Serves 6

MACHO CHICKEN

2 tbsp (30 ml) veggie oil, divided

¼ tsp red pepper flakes

1 Spanish onion, sliced

1 green pepper, sliced

1 yellow pepper, sliced

1 red pepper, sliced

2 tbsp (17 g) garlic, minced

4 plump chicken breasts, skinless, boneless

2 tsp (12 g) salt, divided

1 tsp pepper, divided

½ cup (120 ml) hot sauce (I recommend Frank's RedHot)

2 cups (480 g) of passata (see Flip Tip)

1 tbsp (7 g) smoked paprika

1 tbsp (7 g) cumin

1 tbsp (15 g) white sugar or 2 tbsp (30 ml) honey

MACHO CHEESE

2 tbsp (28 g) salted butter

2 tbsp (16 g) all-purpose flour

1 cup (240 ml) whole milk

3 cups (339 g) shredded medium cheddar cheese

¼ tsp salt

½–1 tsp chili powder

Tortilla chips, to serve (For homemade chips, check out my Homie Chips 'n' Pico de Guaco [page 26])

TOPPERS

Green onions, chopped

2 plum tomatoes, chopped

FLIP TIP: Passata is an uncooked tomato puree, without seeds and skin, that's been salted, bottled, and preserved. Using this raw form of tomato sauce will bring a fresh and bright flavor to the dish.

To make the chicken, add 1 tablespoon (15 ml) of the veggie oil to the empty slow cooker, along with my FAVE, red pepper flakes. Drop in the onion, green, yellow, and red peppers, and the minced garlic.

Season both sides of the chicken with 1 teaspoon of the salt and ½ teaspoon of the pepper. Throw the remaining 1 tablespoon (15 ml) of salt and ½ teaspoon of pepper into the slow cooker with the veggies. Place the chicken on top of the veggies, lining the breasts up side by side. Add the hot sauce, passata, paprika, cumin, sugar, and remaining 1 tablespoon (15 ml) of oil. Cover the pot and set it to cook on high for 4 hours. The dome-shaped lid of the slow cooker is designed to "rain" the moisture back down into the pot, making for a moist dish cooked in its own juices. So don't open the lid to peek in!

FOUR . . . HOURS . . . L . . . A . . . T . . . E . . . R

All right, you guys are on your way to a delicious batch of nachos. How about we get our nacho cheese sauce started?

To make the cheese, melt the butter over medium heat in a small sauce pot, then add the flour to make a little roux. Stir it around to get the raw flour taste out, until it looks like a mushy oatmeal mix—that's exactly what you want. Stir in the milk, whisking until it thickens slightly. Turn off the heat. Add the shredded cheese, ½ cup (57 g) at a time. If it needs a little push to melt, go ahead and turn the heat back on for a few minutes. Once the cheese is melted, add the salt, and lastly the chili powder. Feel free to toss in another ½ teaspoon of chili powder to add more kick—it's a lot of cheese! Mix well. If it gets too thick before serving, add another splash of milk.

Now it's time to open the slow cooker lid to reveal all the yumminess. Transfer the chicken into a large bowl, and shred it. Add three or four big scoops of the sauce and veggie bits from the slow cooker and mix. The rest of the sauce can be used as an extra salsa-like topper for your nachos.

Scoop the chicken-nacho mix into a bowl or onto a serving dish with your tortilla chips. Sometimes I fan out my chips or I like to just poke them through the mixture. Top with chopped green onions and tomatoes and SMOTHER the dish with ladles of nacho cheese sauce. Just thinking of this has my taste buds going nutty. You're finally done, EAT UP!

~ LUMPTY DUMPTY CRAB DIP ~

It takes a ton of restraint for me to not lock my doors and hoard this incredibly delicious appetizer for myself. But one must share, I suppose.

This recipe has been tweaked at least 20 times in my lifetime. That seems like a silly amount of work for an appetizer, right? But trial and error is an important part of the cooking journey. You win some, you burn some, and then by George, you've got it!

First and foremost, lump crabmeat is a must for this recipe. It's plump and juicy and will hold up well during the heating process. My combo of cheeses and sour cream is on point, it's the perfect mix that gives this dip the creamiest texture. This decadent dip is so E-Z to make, by the time you finish slicing up a baguette and arranging it on a pretty little serving tray, hello, it's ready!

Serves 4

1 (8-oz [227-g]) package cream cheese, softened

¼ cup (60 ml) sour cream

¼ cup (60 ml) mayonnaise

1 tsp curry powder

½ tsp Old Bay seasoning

1 tbsp (10 g) white onion, finely chopped

1 tbsp (6 g) celery, finely chopped

2 tbsp (30 ml) ketchup

1 tsp fresh lemon juice

1 lb (454 g) lump crabmeat

¾ cup (85 g) white medium sharp cheddar cheese, grated

¾ cup (85 g) Monterey Jack cheese, grated

1 small green onion, chopped thinly, for garnish

First things first, preheat the oven to 350°F (177°C).

In a large mixing bowl, combine the cream cheese, sour cream, and mayo. Use an electric mixer to cream the mixture together until smooth. Add the curry powder, Old Bay, white onion, celery, ketchup, and lemon juice, and blend until well combined. Use a spatula to fold in the lump crabmeat. Mix the cheddar and Monterey Jack cheeses together in a bowl, then add 1 cup (113 g) into the creamy crab mix.

Scoop the crabmeat mixture into a small casserole dish or cast iron pan. Top with the remaining ½ cup (57 g) of the cheese combo.

Bake on the middle rack for 20 to 25 minutes, until the cheese is melted and the outer rim develops a golden-brown edge. If you're like me and love a nice char on the top of a cheese dip, broil the dish on medium for 2 to 3 minutes.

Garnish with the chopped green onion. Serve right away with a lovely toasted baguette or my favorite cracker, melba toast.

～ MY OH MY, PIZZA PIE ～

I have a distinct memory of the first time pizza was actually made at my house, rather than ordered from a pizza joint. I remember being fascinated that there was a PIZZA being made in MY home, in MY kitchen, in MY own oven. WOWZER! It's fun to have a pizza-making night! Creating your own personal pan pizzas with a simple homemade sauce and a fresh batch of dough is a cooking achievement. Fresh dough is lighter, crispier and tastes so much better than ready-made dough. And, bonus—you'll love the smell of the rising dough!

Yields 3 (10- to 12-inch [25- to 30-cm]) pizzas

DOUGH

2 cups (480 ml) plus 2 tbsp (30 ml) water, room temp

2¼ tsp (10 g) dry yeast, or 1 package

½ tsp honey

3¼ cups (407 g) all-purpose flour, divided, plus additional for work surfaces

2 tbsp (30 g) sea salt

2 tsp (10 ml) olive oil

Sprinkle of cornmeal

SAUCE

1 tbsp (15 ml) olive oil

1 medium onion, grated or finely minced

1 tbsp (7 g) carrot, grated

3 cloves garlic, minced

1 (16-oz [454-g]) can tomato paste

3½ cups (840 ml) passata

2 tbsp (4 g) dried oregano

2 tbsp (4 g) dried basil

1 tsp salt

½ tsp freshly ground black pepper

TOPPERS

Mozzarella, pepperoni, mushrooms, sausage, peppers, onions, fresh basil, anchovies— whatevs, you choose!

Now, if you're anything like me, you probably get a bit nervous with any type of dough making. I'll be honest, it's been a love-hate relationship for me for many years, with many batches scrapped. But now I think I've got it. The main reason that my dough was hit or miss was simply—my YEAST. When things didn't go well, it was either because the yeast was old or because it didn't activate properly. So be sure to check the expiration date on your package.

In an extra-large bowl or tub, combine the water with the yeast. Mix for 2 minutes to dissolve the yeast, then add the honey to activate it. This is called "blooming," for you science folks.

Add 2¼ cups (281 g) of flour to the liquid and mix well. Yes, it will feel as wet and gooey as it looks. Cover the mixture with a clean kitchen towel and let it rest for 20 minutes.

Uncover the dough and add the salt. Mix well, then add the remaining 1 cup (125 g) of flour. You'll need a flat, clean surface to work the dough on, like a table top, cutting board or kitchen counter. Dust this surface with flour as well.

Now's the fun part—it's time to get in there and have some Play-Doh flashbacks! The dough will be very sticky at first, but will start to hold together as you work with it. Add the olive oil and work it through the dough with your hands, then place the dough down on your work surface and start kneading. Push down and through the dough, fold it in towards you, then do a quarter turn and start again. Repeat for a good 15 minutes. This is how gluten is developed for that beautiful, stretchy texture. Phew! You got this, you're a human dough machine. When you're finished kneading, place the dough back into the mixing bowl, cover it, and allow it to rest for 25 more minutes.

(continued)

MY OH MY, PIZZA PIE (Continued)

GREAT JOB SO FAR! Now prep three freezer bags by placing about a teaspoon of flour in each and shaking well to coat the inside of the bag.

Uncover the rested dough and cut it into three strips. Take one strip and fold the sides in and under itself, as if you're forming a mushroom cap, and place it in a floured freezer bag. Repeat two more times. Here's the deal—you have to let these rest from lunch to dinner time, about 5 to 6 hours, preferably in a warm place. Patience is truly a virtue here, but it'll be worth the wait.

What's next? Now's the perfect time to make some homemade pizza sauce if you want to be a true *pizzaiolo*—that's Italian for pizza maker. Start by warming the olive oil in a skillet over low heat. Add the onion, carrot and garlic, and sauté on low heat for a couple of minutes, until the veggies turn translucent. Add the tomato paste, passata, oregano, basil, salt and pepper and mix well. Keep cooking on low for 5 to 7 minutes, until the ingredients are thoroughly mixed and warmed through. Remove the sauce from the heat and let it cool, then store it in the fridge until your dough is ready.

Preheat your oven to 450°F (232°C). If you have a pizza stone or pizza pan, place it in the oven on the rack right below the center. If you don't have one, you can use the back of a baking sheet as a make-shift pizza stone.

Grab your freezer bags and let's get crackin' on the dough. It's best to heavily flour the cutting board before placing down your dough. Then use your knuckles and fingers to spread and stretch the dough—you can make it into the traditional round shape, about 10 to 12 inches (25 to 30 cm) in diameter, or you can make it into a rectangle almost the same size and shape as your cooking tray. Now THROW the dough up in the air with a twisting motion, close your eyes and CATCH it behind your back . . . totally kidding, of course.

If you happen to have a pizza shovel, that's great! If not, you're going to use a second baking sheet as a shovel to transfer the uncooked dough onto the hot tray or stone that's already in the oven.

Cut a piece of parchment paper to the same size as your hot pizza stone or baking sheet that's been flipped over. Dust some cornmeal over the parchment paper, then carefully lay the stretched dough onto it. Spoon and spread a little over ½ to ¾ cup (120 to 180 ml) of pizza sauce onto the dough. Is the cornmeal step absolutely necessarily? Yup, I think so. It will help to properly cook the dough and you'll end up with a crunchy, crispy bottom crust.

Precook the dough with the sauce on the parchment paper for 5 minutes.

Now slide the pizza with the parchment paper out of the oven and back onto the cold baking sheet or shovel. Precook the other two pies in the same fashion.

It's topper time, folks, and my assembly instructions are simple: First, more sauce if you're "that person." Second, your favorite pizza toppings. Here are my three favorite pizza constructions: One with fresh mozzarella, pepperoni slices, and fresh basil, another with mushrooms, sweet Italian sausage, onions, and peppers, and a third with a crazy amount of meat, OH yeahhhh. After the toppers are on, I like to brush the exposed outer crust with a bit of olive oil. This will give the crust those authentic crisp and brown dough bubbles you see on pies coming out of brick ovens.

Bake each pizza for approximately 10 to 12 additional minutes, or until the crust is golden brown and the pepperoni are starting to curl up. Stay near your oven so that you don't burn your amazing creations!

Holy cannoli, can you believe you did it? You've officially earned an A++ in Pizza 101. Save me a slice!

BUBBA'S BEEF 'N' POTATO EGG ROLLS

I created these hearty beef 'n' potato–filled rolls for my niece, Grace, a.k.a. "Bubba." She's my partner-in-crime in the kitchen, always interested in hanging out with me when I cook. I came up with this recipe 'cause my niece loves beef and potatoes, and she was "starving" one day and couldn't wait for me to make a full meal. So I had to be creative and adapt. Luckily, one of the ingredients I had available to substitute and use as a timesaver was leftover mashed potatoes. This recipe quickly became my niece's go-to snack, and is a big hit with the rest of the family too. Just a couple of these satisfying rolls fill me up. Try these instead of a burger and fries—the dipping sauce IS ketchup, after all—or switch it up with either hot Sriracha or my sweet Lucky Ducky Sauce (page 152).

Yields 10 to 12 egg rolls

MASHED POTATOES

4 large russet potatoes, peeled, rinsed, and quartered

1 tbsp (8 g) kosher salt

½ tsp salt

2 tbsp (28 g) salted butter

¼ cup (60 ml) heavy cream, warm

BEEF

2 tbsp (30 ml) veggie oil

½ lb (227 g) ground beef (80% lean, 20% fat is best)

½ tsp salt

1 Spanish onion, chopped

2 cloves garlic, minced

¼ tsp freshly ground black pepper

4 tbsp (60 ml) soy sauce

1 egg

6 tbsp (48 g) all-purpose flour

1 package of large spring roll or egg roll wrappers

4 cups (960 ml) veggie oil

First on the docket is making a batch of mashed taters (unless you have leftovers—then you can skip this step). In a deep pot, add enough cold water to cover an inch above the potatoes. Bring the water to a boil, add the kosher salt, then simmer for 20 minutes. While the taters are simmering, let's get crackin' on the beef.

Grab a large skillet and bring it up to a medium-high heat. Add the veggie oil and watch for it to ripple a bit, that's the signal to add in the ground meat. Sprinkle in the salt and cook about 7 minutes, until the beef is browned.

When the beef is almost fully cooked, add in the onion, garlic, and pepper. Cook about another 5 minutes, until the onion turns translucent and tender. Add the soy sauce, then transfer to a bowl, cover, and cool in the refrigerator for 10 minutes.

This is the perfect time to move back to tater cooking. Drain the potatoes and place them back into the same hot pot. Let them dry for about 5 minutes, allowing the moisture to naturally steam out for a flakier potato. Use a masher, or my fave tool, a fork. No need to get rid of all the lumps. Add the salt, butter, and cream, and mix them into the tater mush.

Now it's time to add in the cooled beef mixture. Using a spatula, gently fold the beef mix into the potatoes.

Scoop the mix into a large sealer bag. Make sure the bag is one that lies flat, with pointy corners—not a gusset bag. Push the mix into one corner of the bag and release all the air before sealing it. We are making a makeshift piping bag. Twist the bag until it's tight, and tie off the part with the mix using a rubber band or twist tie. Cut a 1½-inch (4-cm) long opening in one corner of the bag to create a spout. This will create a meat roll 2 inches (5 cm) in diameter.

(continued)

BUBBA'S BEEF 'N' POTATO EGG ROLLS (Continued)

In a small bowl, whisk the egg and set it aside. This will be the egg wash used to seal the wrappers.

Divide the flour evenly between two baking sheets. One sheet will be your prep surface, and the other is for your wrapped rolls. First, set one wrapper down on the prep sheet with a corner facing you, so that it forms a funny-looking diamond. Starting 2 inches (5 cm) from the left corner, squeeze the meat mixture onto the wrapper. Try to keep your squeezing consistent, so the mixture comes out in a continuous 2-inch (5-cm) roll, and stop squeezing when you're 2 inches (5 cm) from the right corner. Take both the left and right corners and fold them over the mixture as if wrapping a gift box. Be sure to wrap tightly, otherwise you'll end up with a pan of floating filling and broken wrappers! Now take the corner closest to you and fold that tightly over the filling, being careful not to tear the wrapper. Dip your finger into the egg wash and coat the last corner, the one farthest away from you. Fold the coated corner over the filling to seal the wrapper. Place the completed roll, sealed side down, onto the second floured baking sheet. Continue the rolling steps until you have your 10 to 12 rolls.

In a medium-sized pot, heat the oil over low to medium heat—you want the rolls to brown slowly. I like to deep fry only three rolls at a time so they don't crowd the pot and cool the oil temperature. Keep an eye on the egg rolls, as the wrapper browns quite easily. Turn them over and over to make sure the entire roll is getting golden brown. Cooking time is short, 3 to 4 minutes.

Grab the rolls out with tongs and place them in a strainer vertically to properly drain excess oil. Let them cool for a few minutes before eating, and don't forget the ketchup!

~ HOMIE CHIPS 'N' PICO DE GUACO ~

My homemade tortilla chips, pico de gallo and guacamole are definitely influenced by my numerous trips to Cancùn in my crazy youth. And my soft spot for some good chips 'n' salsa any time of day is probably from all the bar snacks I've devoured while stuck in airports during my travels. As you'll learn from this recipe, making homemade chips is extremely satisfying, and it will boost your cooking confidence. Plus, food cooked from scratch is always better than store bought. Here goes!

Yields 5 dozen chips, 2 cups (544 g) of pico de gallo, 3 cups (720 g) of guacamole

PICO DE GALLO

½ small red onion, diced

4 plum tomatoes, seeded and diced

2 jalapeños, diced, optional to leave seeds in for an extra kick, or to use a hotter pepper like a Serrano

1 clove garlic, minced

4 tbsp (60 ml) fresh lime juice

1 tbsp (4 g) fresh parsley, chopped

2 tsp (2 g) cilantro or 1 tsp dill

1 tsp salt, plus more to taste

Pinch of freshly ground black pepper

GUACAMOLE

2 ripe avocados, scooped out and mashed (see Flip Tip)

¼ tsp salt, plus more to taste

2 tbsp (30 ml) fresh lime juice

1 cup (272 g) of your Pico de Gallo

TORTILLA CHIPS

½ cup (114 g) melted butter

1 tsp white or black pepper

1 tsp cumin

1 tsp onion powder

1 tsp garlic powder

1 tsp cayenne pepper

1 tsp lime zest

8 (8-inch [20-cm]) white flour or corn tortillas, each cut into 8 triangles

To make the pico de gallo, mix the onion, tomatoes, jalapeños, garlic, lime juice, parsley, cilantro, and salt and pepper in a medium bowl.

For the guac, combine the avocados, salt, lime juice, and pico de gallo in another medium bowl. You can always add more lime juice and salt to taste—I do!

Now it's time to preheat the oven to 350°F (177°C).

Place cooling racks or parchment paper on top of two baking sheets. Combine the butter, pepper, cumin, onion powder, garlic powder, cayenne pepper, and zest on a shallow plate. Dip the tortilla triangles in the mixture to coat each chip. Let the excess drip off, and arrange the chips in one layer on the racks.

Bake the chips for 15 minutes at 350°F (177°C). If you're using parchment paper, bake 5 to 7 minutes longer, 20 to 22 minutes total, to ensure you get golden brown and crispy chips.

If the chips are too greasy, blot them with paper towels. For saltier chips, sprinkle on more salt while they're hot. Serve with the pico and guac.

FLIP TIP: To test an avocado for ripeness, press down on the end of the avocado with your finger. If it goes back to its original shape when you remove your finger, that's a good fruit. If it stays depressed, that one's really ripe, but you can still use it if you mix it with one that's not so overly ripe.

When it comes to crab cakes, lump crabmeat is an absolute must. There are fine and dandy recipes out there using claw meat, but it's a completely different taste—a bit fishy if you ask me. Instead, ask your local fish monger if he has any fresh lump crabmeat stashed away, or at the very least see if you can find cans of lump crabmeat in the seafood section of your grocery store. It's a little more expensive, but HEY, your taste buds are absolutely worth it. Special occasions don't have to be your only time to splurge! Prep Aioli Moli (page 164), Lady Remoulade (page 167) or even Fools 'n' Sauces (page 160) prior to cooking for a perfect finish.

Yields 4 to 6 large cakes

CAKES

¼ cup (60 ml) mayo

2 tbsp (30 ml) fresh lemon juice

1 tsp lemon zest

1 tbsp (15 ml) Dijon mustard

1 tsp Worcestershire sauce

1 tsp Old Bay seasoning

1 tsp garlic powder

¼ tsp salt

¼ tsp freshly ground black pepper

¼ tsp cayenne pepper

2 whole green onions, chopped

1 tbsp (4 g) fresh parsley, chopped

2 tbsp (28 g) salted butter, melted

½ cup (35 g) Ritz crackers, crushed

¼ cup (14 g) Panko Japanese-style breadcrumbs

1 lb (454 g) lump crabmeat

2 tbsp (16 g) cornstarch

½ cup (63 g) all-purpose flour

1 tsp garlic powder, optional

¼ cup (60 ml) veggie oil

TOPPERS

1 tbsp (15 ml) fresh cilantro, chopped

1 tbsp (15 ml) fresh dill, chopped

1 tbsp (3 g) fresh chives, chopped

To make the cakes, whisk this lovely family of ingredients together in a medium-sized bowl: mayonnaise, lemon juice, lemon zest, mustard, Worcestershire sauce, Old Bay, garlic powder, salt, black pepper, and, last but not least, cayenne pepper. Mix in the chopped green onions and fresh parsley.

In a separate bowl, combine the melted butter, crackers, and breadcrumbs. Add this mix to the original family of ingredients. Terrific, so far so good! Now use a spatula to gingerly fold in the plump, lump crabmeat. Place in the fridge for 10 minutes.

Mix up the cornstarch, flour and garlic powder if you're using it. This coating ensures a crispy crust when frying.

Set out two plates. Use one for the formed patties, and line the other with a paper towel for draining the finished fried crab cakes.

Next, grab the mixture from the fridge and use a ¼-cup (60-ml) measuring scoop to form the crab mix into patties. Dredge each patty in the flour and cornstarch, and set them aside on the first plate. Repeat until all four to six patties are formed.

Heat the oil in a skillet over medium-high heat. Place 3 or 4 patties in at a time, and fry for 3 to 4 minutes on each side, until a beautiful, crispy brown coating is formed. Place the finished cakes on the paper towel–lined plate to remove the excess oil before plating.

Top with some cilantro, dill, and chives. Chef's choice to serve it up with one or more of my sauces for the perfect dunk!

Veggies Galore

Corn, squash, green beans, and cabbage,
Cucumber, eggplant, and carrots are savage.
No need to hide 'em, drowned in a sauce,
You name it, I'll eat it, sautéed like a boss.

As a kid, I always liked my veggies! But sadly, there are folks out there who don't eat vegetables at all, because get this—THEY JUST DON'T KNOW HOW TO COOK THEM! Eeks, not on my watch. Never fear, for this chapter I've dug up a bunch of fun and E-Z-to-follow recipes to help you explore a variety of different ways to "veg out." I hope that these dishes grow to become some of your family favorites!

⸺ BEETS AN EVERYDAY SALAD ⸺
(WITH FRIED RICE NOODLES)

I've been trying to remember the first time I ate this salad. All I recall is that I was a kid at a big party, and that when I spotted itty bitty plates of colorful veggies topped with crispy fried rice noodles I said, "Ooooo, what the heck is that?" I was shocked to learn it was a SALAD, and even more shocked by how much I liked it! It was over the top with its tangy, sweet sesame dressing and crunchy fried rice noodles.

Over the years, I've tweaked the ingredients of this recipe by adding chunks of chicken, and, wait for it . . . BEETS! I know, right? Raw beets are earthy and slightly bitter, but cooking them brings out a mild sweetness that's quite delicious. Cooking also gives them a crisp, tender texture. For this recipe, I've paired the beets with fresh flavors of sweet mandarin oranges and tangy grapefruit to give the salad a nice balance. The crunchy fried noodles give it a fun texture combo in every bite. Top it off with my Asian Persuasion Dressing (page 156) for a salad of sweet sesame and garlic flavors you'll want to eat every day.

I have to give credit to my brother-in-law, Simon, for introducing me to beets. He also happens to be a pretty darn good cook . . . at least that's what my family tells him. Just kidding, thanks, Si!

Serves 4 to 6

3 chicken breasts with skin on, optional

Salt, divided

Freshly ground black pepper

6 medium-sized beets, scrubbed

2 tbsp (30 ml) apple cider vinegar

2 cups (480 ml) veggie oil

3 handfuls of crispy rice noodles

1 head of iceberg lettuce, cored and chopped

1 head of romaine lettuce, cored and chopped

1 cup (70 g) red cabbage, cored and finely shredded

1 cup (110 g) carrots, shredded

1 can Mandarin orange segments, drained

½ cup (48 g) green onions, thinly sliced

Asian Persuasion Dressing (page 156)

1 tbsp (9 g) sesame seeds

Grapefruit segments, optional

Blood orange segments, optional

Poached shrimp, optional

Preheat your oven to 450°F (232°C).

There are three E-Z peasy ingredients to cook for this recipe. We're starting with the chicken since it has the longest cooking time, 40 to 50 minutes, but do note that adding chicken is optional. This salad tastes terrific without any proteins added.

Season the chicken breasts with salt and pepper. Then, do it again. Now you know what it means when recipes state to season "liberally."

Place the chicken on a foil-lined baking sheet and bake uncovered for 40 to 50 minutes. The chicken is done when the internal temperature of the thickest part of the meat reads at least 165°F (74°C). You'll only know that if you have a meat thermometer, so get one! Let the chicken cool, then cut it into bite-sized cubes, keeping the skin on.

Drop the beets into a large pot with the skin on. Fill the pot with cold water, to about 2 inches (5 cm) above the submerged beets. Add the apple cider vinegar. This helps reduce the funky odor that beets give off when they're boiled, and it helps retain their deep red color and bring out their freshness. Boil for 30 minutes.

When the 30 minutes are up, scoop out the beets and submerge them in an ice bath. Once they're cool, peel them, using gloves to avoid hand stains (or ask someone else to do it!). Slice into ½-inch (1.3-cm) cuts.

(continued)

BEETS AN EVERYDAY SALAD (WITH FRIED RICE NOODLES)
(Continued)

The third ingredient to cook is the rice noodles. In a big pot or frying pan, add in your oil, and bring the heat up to high. Separate the noodles into manageable batches. This can be done by using a pair of kitchen shears. Grab a handful of noodles and place them in the hot oil. In 3 to 4 minutes, BOOM! The rice noodles will fry, puff up, and expand. It's quite fun to see. Scoop them up and drain them on paper towels. Sprinkle them with a pinch of salt, and you're ready to plate up.

On a large serving platter or in a large bowl, combine the lettuces, cabbage, carrots, Mandarin orange, and green onions. Pour in one-third of the Asian Persuasion Dressing. Toss the salad a couple of times, then top it off with the fried rice noodles and sesame seeds. Add the grapefruit, blood orange, and poached shrimp, if using, and always serve with the remaining dressing on the side.

You will love this salad combo. You can't BEET it!

~ VEGGIE ROLLEE POLLEEZ ~
(EGG ROLLS)

Filipinos love feeding people, even when they're not hungry. I remember always having a ridiculous amount of food at Filipino gatherings. The staple food at any party is the never-ending tray of egg rolls. Vegetable egg rolls are usually special occasion rolls, but I started making them regularly as a salad substitute. My nieces actually like them, even though they're full of veggies. Hey, they're E-Z to eat and just so good dunked in the special sauce. Of course, I've got that for you too—try these veggie rolls with my Flip Dip (page 159) or my sweet 'n' sour Lucky Ducky Sauce (page 152)!

Yields 10 to 12 egg rolls

8 shiitake mushrooms, fresh preferred	4 large cloves garlic, minced
4 cups (960 ml) plus 2 tbsp (30 ml) veggie oil, divided	½ tsp salt
¼ tsp red pepper flakes	¼ tsp freshly ground black pepper
1 large Spanish onion, sliced (white onions or shallots are also great)	3 green onions, chopped (see Flip Tip)
1 large carrot, grated or finely chopped	1 tsp sesame oil, hot or original
1 cup (110 g) green beans, chopped on the bias	1 egg
2 cups (140 g) green cabbage, sliced into thin ribbons	6 tbsp (48 g) all-purpose flour, divided
½ small red cabbage, sliced into thin ribbons	1 package egg roll or spring roll wrappers

First up are the shiitake mushrooms. If you're using fresh mushrooms, you can skip this step. If you're using dried, they need to be hydrated, so: Place the shrooms in simmering water for 10 minutes, then drain and cool. Cut off the stems. We don't want to use them because they're too tough to eat. Slice the caps and set aside.

Heat your wok over medium heat. Add 2 tablespoons (30 ml) of the veggie oil and my go-to fave, red pepper flakes. Start by adding the Spanish onion, sauté and sweat it without letting it brown. This is followed by the carrot, green beans, cabbage, garlic, salt, and pepper. Mix them together and sauté for 5 minutes.

Add the shhhiiiiiTAKE (Gesundheit!) mushrooms, green onions, and sesame oil. Mix and sauté for another 5 minutes, until all the veggies have cooked and are wilted.

Scoop the veggies out and place them into a large strainer bowl, making sure to capture all the juices into another bowl underneath. Do not discard the drippings, reserve them to add to the Flip Dip (page 159) sauce. Mix occasionally to ensure proper drainage, and cool for 5 minutes. It's important to drain as much of the juices as possible so you don't have soggy egg rolls.

Once it's cooled, scoop the mix into a large sealer bag. Make sure the bag is one that lies flat, with pointy corners—not a gusset bag. Push the mix into one corner of the bag and release all the air before sealing. We are making a makeshift piping bag. Twist the bag until it's tight and tie off the part with the mix using a rubber band or twist tie. Cut a 1½-inch (4-cm) opening in the corner of the bag to create a spout. This will create a veggie roll 2 inches (5 cm) in diameter.

(continued)

VEGGIE ROLLEE POLLEEZ (EGG ROLLS)
(Continued)

In a small bowl, whisk the egg and set it aside. This will be the egg wash used to seal the wrappers.

Divide the flour evenly between two baking sheets. One sheet will be your prep surface and the other is for your wrapped rolls. First, set one wrapper down with a corner facing you, so that it forms a funny-looking diamond. Starting 2 inches (5 cm) from the left corner, squeeze the veggies onto the wrapper. Try to keep your squeezing consistent, so the mixture comes out in a continuous 2-inch (5-cm) roll, and stop squeezing when you're 2 inches (5 cm) from the right corner. Take both the left and right corners and fold them over the veggie mixture as if wrapping a gift box. Be sure to wrap tightly, otherwise you'll end up with a pan of floating filling and broken wrappers! Now take the corner closest to you and fold that tightly over the filling, being careful not to tear the wrapper. Dip your finger into the egg wash and coat the last corner, the one farthest away from you. Fold the coated corner over the filling to seal the wrapper. Place the completed roll sealed side down onto your second floured baking sheet. Continue the rolling steps until you have your 10 to 12 rolls. See page 25 for some photos of this process.

In a large pot or skillet, heat the remaining veggie oil over low to medium heat. You want the rolls to brown slowly. I like to deep-fry only three at a time so they don't overcrowd the pot and cool the oil temperature. You must keep an eye on the egg rolls, as the wrappers brown quite easily. Turn them over and over to make sure the entire roll is getting golden brown. Cooking time is short, 3 to 4 minutes.

Grab the rolls out with tongs and place them in a strainer vertically to properly drain excess oil. Let them cool for a few minutes.

Cut the cooled rolls in half on the bias (at an angle) to display the beautiful array of mixed vegetables inside. Serve with the Flip Dip (page 159) or Lucky Ducky Sauce (page 152).

It's the tastiest salad-in-a-roll you'll ever have!

FLIP TIP: Green onions and scallions are literally the same thing. Spring onions, however, are different. They have a distinct bulb at the root end that green onions/scallions don't.

UNCLE VINNIE'S ALMOST-FAMOUS POTATO SALAD

Hello, potato salad lovers! You're in for a treat with this family fave. The key to a winning potato salad is using the perfect potato, and waxy Yukon Gold is the one for this job. It holds its shape during the cooking process, and keeps its firm texture when mixed with all the fixings. What makes my recipe unique is that I incorporated a hot, buttery dressing into a cold salad. Also, just the right blend of apple cider vinegar and both Dijon and grainy mustards makes this particular recipe a hit at first bite.

Thanks to my brother Vinnie for the bones of this recipe. His version was a tough one to beat, but it's always fun to take a good, solid recipe and add your personal flair to it!

Serves 8 to 10

POTATO SALAD

4 lb (1.8 kg) Yukon Gold potatoes, skin on

3 tbsp (24 g) plus a pinch of kosher salt, divided

Pinch of pepper

1 tsp white distilled vinegar

7 eggs

3 celery ribs, chopped

1 medium red onion, chopped

3 tbsp (45 g) sweet relish

HOT DRESSING

2 tbsp (28 g) butter

1¼ cups (250 g) white sugar

⅓ cup (80 ml) apple cider vinegar

1 tsp Dijon mustard

1 tsp grainy mustard

1 tsp salt

5 eggs

2 cups (480 ml) mayo

TOPPERS

2 tbsp (7 g) paprika, for color and presentation (smoked paprika is a nice touch)

Crispy bacon bits

Green onions, chopped

Walnuts, chopped

Poached shrimp, shelled, deveined, chilled, optional

Start by using a 5-quart (4.7-L) stock pot filled with 3 quarts (2.8 L) of cold water. Add the potatoes and kosher salt. Bring to a boil, then reduce to a simmer for 15 to 20 minutes, until the potatoes are easily fork tender. Use a large slotted spoon to scoop up the potatoes, and strain them. Lay them out in a single layer on a baking sheet lined with paper towels to continue to dry. Give them a little pinch of salt and pepper.

Let's be efficient and pull double duty by using the same pot of water to cook up some hard-boiled eggs. Add 1 teaspoon of vinegar to help make them easier to peel. Bring the water and vinegar to a boil, drop in the eggs, and cook for 8 to 9 minutes. Once they've cooled, chop them up into small cubes.

Cube the dried potatoes, and combine them in a large bowl with the celery, red onion, relish, and chopped eggs, then set aside.

To put together the hot dressing, it's best to use a small sauce pan. Start by slowly melting the butter on low heat. Use a whisk to mix in the sugar, apple cider vinegar, Dijon and grainy mustards, salt, and eggs, adding the eggs last. Simmer for 5 to 7 minutes while continuously whisking. The eggs will gradually cook, much like a hollandaise sauce cooks on indirect heat, but the consistency will be quite thin and liquid-y. Take them off the heat. Now it's time to beat in the mayonnaise, which will thicken the egg sauce.

Pour the hot dressing mix into the potato-veggie bowl, and combine.

Decorate by sprinkling on some paprika. You can jazz it up with the bacon bits, green onions, and walnuts, but if you REALLY want to show off, make sure to add in some shrimp! I expect you to be invited to ALL the BBQs after sharing this dish.

FRESH FRIES PLEASE, I'LL WAIT!

Have you ever had a craving for some crispy, piping hot fast-food fries? Of course you have, who hasn't? One of the worst feelings is when you order them at a drive thru, and just as you pull away, you realize you've been given soggy old fries. What the hell?! The last time this happened to me, I told myself, "Never again." Ever since that time, I always roll up to the intercom and make sure I order properly: "Fresh fries, please . . . Yes, I'll wait."

With this surefire recipe, you can make a batch of homemade fries any time you want, ensuring that they're always fresh and crispy. For some additional deliciousness, try topping them with my Cheez LOeez! (page 163). Told ya, never again!

Serves 4

8 medium russet potatoes

1½ cups (188 g) all-purpose flour

¾ cup (96 g) cornstarch

4 cups (960 ml) veggie oil

Salt, to taste

With the skins on, submerge the potatoes in a pot of cold water. Bring to a boil, then reduce the heat and simmer for ONLY 10 minutes. Yes, I said 10 minutes. This is called a "parboil," meaning "partially cooked by boiling" in chef talk.

Drain the potatoes and let them cool on a cutting board for a few minutes. Cut them lengthwise into fries. Thick fries are basically four times the size of shoestring fries. This is a safe size to cut the parboiled potatoes so they hold their shape and don't break.

Mix the flour and cornstarch together, then dredge the cut-up potatoes.

Fill up a deep pot with 4 cups (960 ml) of oil (or whatever amount of oil you're comfortable using). Heat the oil to 375°F (190°C), using an oil thermometer to verify the temperature. Fry the potatoes for 5 to 10 minutes, cooking in batches so that the pan isn't overcrowded. Also, allow the oil to come back up to 375°F (190°C) between batches. You're looking for the fries to turn a deep golden brown, and for the skins of the potatoes to look crisp and flaky. Season with salt straight away.

Serve with ketchup, malt vinegar, or my Cheez LOeez! (page 163).

～ GIMMIE GARLIC CORN ～

Gimme Garlic Corn was E-Z pickins when I was deciding on a name for my garlic corn dish. Sautéing corn brings out its natural sugars, which makes it very appealing to your taste buds, and adding garlic to the sauté ramps up the flavor and adds complexity to a simple recipe. It's a savory side dish for any meal, but it's especially perfect for BBQs.

I'm sure a bunch of you folks have fond memories of attending family get-togethers. Remember how there was always an overabundance of food, and everyone wanted you to take a scoop of their "famous" potluck dish? Well, I was the baby of the clan and a growing boy, so I was the perfect guinea pig who got asked to taste EVERYTHING. Picture me being asked what I wanted to eat by every aunt, uncle, and cousin, then multiply that times a thousand, 'cause Filipinos call EVERYONE your aunt, uncle, or cousin, regardless of whether you're related or not! My plate was piled high with a little bit of everybody's creations, but the one thing I distinctly remember asking for was the garlic corn my Momma brought!

In a large nonstick skillet, heat the oil over medium-high heat. Add the garlic, and immediately follow it with the corn. Season with salt and pepper. Mix and sauté for 7 minutes. The garlic aroma should be wafting through the kitchen. The sauté will also make a sizzling, crackling sound, which is absolutely what you want to hear. It's the moisture and natural sugars from the corn being pulled out.

Lower the heat, add the cilantro and/or green onions, if using, and sauté for 3 more minutes. Be sure to test the seasoning and add more salt and pepper if needed. Serve with a squeezed wedge of lemon or lime for a bright citrus taste. GIMME SOME, ALREADY!

Serves 4 to 6

2 tbsp (30 ml) olive oil	¼ tsp freshly ground black pepper
8 cloves garlic, minced	8 leaves of fresh cilantro, chopped, optional
1 (24-oz [680-g]) bag of frozen corn nibblets, or 8 ears of fresh corn, cut off from the cob	2 green onions, diced, optional
½ tsp salt	Lemon or lime wedge, to serve

~ ROOM FOR SHROOMS ~

No matter how stuffed my plate is, or my belly for that matter, I always have room for shrooms. Mushrooms are one of my favorite veggies in the world. There are so many different, funky-looking varieties to try, I highly recommend foraging as many as you can, but for stuffed mushrooms, button and cremini hold up perfectly. For this recipe, I went with the good ol' white button ones. I know stuffed caps are usually served as an appetizer, but I like to have them as part of the main meal. Either way, they're definitely delish!

Yields 48 stuffed caps

48 extra-large white button mushrooms	1 small green pepper, minced
1 cup (164 g) chickpeas, strained	4 cloves garlic, minced
6 tbsp (90 ml) olive oil, divided	1 tbsp (15 ml) fresh lemon juice
¼ tsp salt, plus more to taste	1 (8-oz [227-g]) package of cream cheese, room temp
⅛ tsp freshly ground black pepper, plus more to taste	4 tbsp (60 ml) mayo
1 tsp cayenne pepper	⅓ cup (33 g) plus 2 tbsp (13 g) Parmesan cheese, freshly grated, divided
1 lb (454 g) hot Italian sausage, ground	2 green onions, finely chopped, optional
1 medium onion, minced	2 tbsp (2 g) fresh parsley, chopped, optional

FLIP TIP: If you have any stuffing mixture left over, freeze it to use in a meatloaf or meatball recipe later. I promise you'll like it!

Preparation is simple, but please be gentle, you don't want to break the caps. Wipe the mushrooms with a damp paper towel and gently snap the stems off. Finely chop the stems, they'll be going into the stuffing mixture. Set aside the caps for later.

I love chickpeas! In this dish, they'll be used as a binder instead of the usual breadcrumbs. A binder helps food keep its shape, and adds texture and moisture.

In a medium-sized skillet, sauté the strained chickpeas in 1 tablespoon (15 ml) of the olive oil, over medium heat, for 10 to 15 minutes, until the skin crisps up a bit. Transfer them to a shallow plate and season them with the salt, black pepper, and cayenne pepper. Set them aside to cool.

It's time to preheat the oven to 350°F (177°C).

Crumble the sausage with your hands before adding it to the same skillet you cooked the chickpeas in. Heat the skillet over medium heat, and continue to break up the sausage with a wooden spoon while it cooks to brown, about 5 minutes. With a slotted spoon, scoop out the sausage and transfer it to a bowl. Also set this aside to cool.

Place the onion, green pepper, and garlic into the rendered oils from the sausage. Sauté until the vegetables are tender, about 5 minutes. Add the chopped mushroom stems you saved, then season with salt and pepper to taste. Add the lemon juice in last, then cook for another 5 minutes and set the veggies aside to cool.

In a large mixing bowl, use a fork to combine and smash together the cream cheese, mayo, ⅓ cup (33 g) of Parmesan cheese, and chickpeas. Fold in the cooled cooked sausage, mushroom stem mix, and veggie sauté.

You're almost ready to stuff. Line a baking sheet with parchment paper, or you can use aluminum foil greased with 1 tablespoon (15 ml) of olive oil. Arrange the mushroom caps on the prepped baking sheet. Dress the naked caps with the remaining 4 tablespoons (60 ml) of olive oil and season with salt and pepper. Now use a teaspoon to scoop the stuffing mixture into each cap. Top with the additional 2 tablespoons (13 g) of Parmesan cheese.

Place the baking sheet on the top rack and bake for 25 to 30 minutes. A little moisture will form around each mushroom, which is a good sign that yumminess is happening. Top the baked caps with finely chopped green onions or parsley and serve. Shrooms are up! GET IN MY BELLY!

~ CHEEZY SPUDS ~

It's funny, I've been calling this baked, cheesy dish "scalloped potatoes" since forever, but people say that my particular recipe is actually "potatoes au gratin." Whatevs, it's Cheezy Spuds in my lingo. The recipes are similar, but throughout the years, my potato slices have morphed from a thin one-eighth-inch (3-mm) sliced "scallop" into a thicker half-inch (1.3-cm) "chunk," 'cause I like a bigger bite. AND . . . I've added cheese, why wouldn't I?!

Serves 6

5 cloves garlic, minced

1 tbsp (15 ml) olive oil

2 tbsp (28 g) salted butter, plus more to grease the pan

2 tbsp (15 g) flour

2 cups (480 ml) heavy cream

1 (12-oz [350-ml]) can evaporated milk

2½–3 lb (1.1–1.4 kg) potatoes, peeled and cut into ½-inch (1.3-cm) slices (I prefer russet)

1 cup (100 g) Parmesan cheese, divided

What's the first thing I do when baking? Gather all my ingredients, preheat my oven, and prepare my baking dish. Ingredients . . . check! Preheat oven to 350°F (177°C) . . . check! Grease up my large Dutch oven with a lid . . . check! No aluminum foil needed.

All right, let's get to the creamy, cheesy sauce. In a medium-sized pot, slowly sauté the garlic in olive oil on low heat. Do NOT brown it, just cook it a minute until fragrant. Add in the butter until it melts, then the flour, and continuously whisk to combine. Cook for 3 to 4 minutes, until a tan-colored paste forms, which will be used as a thickener, called a "roux." Sounds fancy, but it's just simply cooking equal parts of flour and fat together. Pour in the heavy cream and evaporated milk and whisk to combine with the roux. Simmer on low for 5 minutes. We're using very little flour, so the roux will thicken the cream. Other ingredients, such as the starch in the potatoes, heavy cream, and evaporated milk, all work together to thicken the sauce when it bakes.

My recipe calls for 2½ to 3 pounds (1.1 to 1.4 kg) of potatoes, which is approximately six to eight spuds. These are starchy, and will help thicken the cream and will bake up nice and tender. No need to submerge them in water to keep them from browning, if you've heard that trick. I don't want any excess water being absorbed, or the cream will end up watery. Add the slices into the heated cream, and simmer for 10 minutes on low heat. I like this step of partially cooking the potatoes before I place them into the oven because it shortens the baking time.

After simmering for 10 minutes, take the potatoes off the heat. Add ⅔ cup (66 g) of Parmesan by carefully folding the cheese into the cream and potatoes, then transfer the mix into the baking dish. Top it off with the remaining ⅓ cup (33 g) of Parmesan and cover with the lid.

Bake for 25 minutes, then uncover. Turn the oven to medium broil for 10 minutes for a beautiful brown and charred top layer. If you only have a setting of high broil, broil for 5 minutes.

This is a PERFECTO side for any meal or special gathering. May I suggest a few of my Carnivorous Cravings: I Spy a Ribeye (page 73) or Smokey LO's Grilled Chicken 'n' Pork (page 52). It's no secret that anything with cheese wins the prize in my eyes.

E-Z ROASTED "VEGGEEZ"

You need some veggies? I'll tell ya an E-Z way to cook some up. These are the four veggies that I first learned how to roast. It's a good start for beginners to become confident in roasting, and also a good place for the more advanced cooks to expand their palette and begin playing with different spices to enhance flavors. For example, in this recipe I use the basics—garlic, oil, salt, and pepper. You can bump it up with red pepper flakes, soy sauce, and sesame oil. I provided the different cook times for a variety of veggies for simple oven roasting at 400°F (204°C). Take your pick. I'm going for a combo of two of my Momma's favorites, asparagus and cauliflower, but they're all fantastico!

Serves 6

½ tsp salt	1½ lb (680 g) thick asparagus spears
¼ tsp freshly ground black pepper	6 russet potatoes, optional
1 head of garlic, cloves separated, peeled, roughly chopped	1 medium head broccoli, optional
6 tbsp (90 ml) olive oil, divided	¼ cup (56 g) salted butter, melted, optional
1 small head cauliflower, cut into bite-sized florets	¼ cup (27 g) almond slivers, optional

Preheat the oven to 400°F (204°C).

In a large bowl, combine the salt, pepper, garlic, and 3 tablespoons (45 ml) of the olive oil. Set aside.

Place the cauliflower florets in a large bowl, and pour half of the oil mixture on top. Toss and mix well. Let that rest for a sec.

Next is the asparagus. I prefer asparagus about as thick as a pencil, 'cause the Pixy Stix–thin ones cook way too fast for my liking. Trim the asparagus by holding the butt end and middle of one spear, then bend it until it snaps off. The bottom end that snapped off is the chewy, woody portion; discard that yucky part. Line up the rest of the asparagus and trim them off at the same area for each spear. In the bowl with the remaining oil mix, toss in the asparagus. Mix well to coat.

On an aluminum baking sheet, spread the cauli-florets all around. I specifically use an aluminum sheet because glass or ceramic baking dishes get too hot and result in burning or overcooking the veggies. Bake the cauliflower on the middle rack for 10 to 15 minutes. Take the pan out of the oven, then speckle the asparagus over the cauliflower. Put it back in the oven for 10 to 15 more minutes, and you're done.

If you like potatoes and broccoli, it's a similar process. Preheat the oven to 400°F (204°C). Cut the potatoes into bite-sized pieces. Break up the broccoli into florets. Toss each veggie in separate bowls with half the olive oil mixture.

Potatoes will be first to go into the oven. Lay them out onto an aluminum sheet. These will bake for 30 minutes. Next, spread the broccoli over the potatoes, and bake the combo for 25 more minutes. Add salt and pepper if needed. It's really that simple folks.

Serve with optional toppers of drizzled melted butter and slivers of almonds. You can always mix and match or do them all, just follow the corresponding cooking times. Give it a shot, and I promise these veggies will grow on ya!

Carnivorous Cravings

Let me preface this chapter by stating that I am a meat and potatoes guy. I love hearty meals filled with meats and carbs. So it was important for me to learn how to cook all types of meat dishes, and you know what, it's not that tricky. Basically when I'm really HUNGRY, I crave meat—and when I crave it, I cook it. It would be rude if I didn't listen to my belly. Momma taught me to be polite, folks.

I compiled these family-friendly, E-Z-to-cook meals to share what I've learned through the years. I show you how to use basic ingredients with a variety of meats, providing you with tips and techniques on how to make them juicy and tender. I've tweaked some classic recipes and added an Asian flair, including a couple of grilled meats, 'cause you just can't beat the smokey taste of sizzling meats hot off the grill.

As you peruse these pages, keep in mind that you'll probably find more than a recipe or two that really whets your whistle. It's all good, go right ahead and give in, whether your craving is for Smokey LO's Grilled Chicken 'n' Pork (page 52), or my Filipino beef stew, Tita Kitty's *Mechado* (page 55). I guarantee that any of these meals will satisfy your desire for meat. I'm sure your momma taught you well too!

SMOKEY LO'S GRILLED CHICKEN 'N' PORK

Many families have a secret recipe for their meat marinade, as they should. It's typically passed down under lock and key, with the precise instructions never to be divulged to outsiders, leaving them to guess what they're tasting. This dish is perfect for a big gathering. Now that we're friends, we're family, so . . . the secret to my Smokey LO's Grilled Chicken 'n' Pork is in THE MARINATION!

Serves 8

2 heads of garlic, crushed

2 large onions, sliced

3 tsp (9 g) whole peppercorns

4 cups (960 ml) soy sauce

1¼ cups (300 ml) white distilled vinegar

2 tsp (4 g) powdered ginger or 2–3-inch (5–8-cm) nub of fresh ginger, grated

½ cup (100 g) sugar

4 cups (960 ml) of any type of soda—7 UP, Sprite, Ginger Ale, or the Flip preferred Coca-Cola

2–3 whole chickens, cut up

8–12 THICK CUT pork chops (I also like country ribs or cut up pork butt)

Get yourself two large bins, a couple of your largest pots, or perhaps grab two of those humongous freezer bags. Any of these will work great as a vessel for the marinade. Combine the garlic, onions, peppercorns, soy sauce, vinegar, ginger, sugar, and soda together, and mix well. The soda carbonation helps the marinade penetrate and flavor the meat all the way through. It also provides sugar, and works with the soy sauce to coat the meat. This results in a dark brown, sweet and tangy skin, and darkens those awesome grill marks. Those marks make your food look tasty, and of course it makes you look like you know what you're doing.

You'll need separate marination containers for the two meats. Completely submerge the chicken and pork into the secret mix. Keep refrigerated for no less than 2 to 3 hours.

Preheat the oven to 350°F (177°C). OK guys, here's another trick to make you look like a grill master. The extra step of precooking the chicken in the oven is needed prior to grilling. Chicken takes longer to cook on the grill than pork. Timing is key, 'cause you want both meats ready to serve at the same time. You don't want to keep your hungry guests waiting or let your hot food get cold. You know that happens all the time. On a baking sheet, lay out the chicken and bake for 45 minutes. This will render some juices that can be used to baste when you're grilling.

It's time to get grillin'! Set your grill to the highest temp. You can now grill batches of both the chicken and pork at the same time. Brush or spoon on some of the corresponding marinade to baste each batch once or twice on each side during the cooking time. They should finish cooking in about 5 to 10 minutes.

Be prepared, 'cause after you serve this up hot on a platter, you will be dubbed the new "Family Grill Master," and be asked to host EVERY family get together . . . until the end of time. You have been warned.

~ TITA KITTY'S *MECHADO* ~
(BEEF 'N' POTATO STEW)

This truly is a family favorite, terrific any time of year. My sister, or Tita (Aunt) Kitty as everyone calls her, made this dish for me every time I visited. Either it's her favorite dish to cook, or the only meal she knows how to cook! But seriously, it doesn't matter 'cause I love it. I remember when I was little and was told we were having it for dinner, a gigantisaurus smile always came across my face. But who am I kidding, I still react the same way.

Mechado is similar to a pot roast–style stew. It's hearty, and has a rich gravy with a mix of beef, potatoes, and veggies. I tweaked it by creating a perfect base of rich tomato sauce, beef stock, and soy sauce. I added a side of green peppers and onions, sautéed with a bit of heat from my favorite spice, red pepper flakes, along with chunks of crispy fried potatoes. You will love this one!

Serves 6

2 lb (900 g) chuck roast, preferably bone-in with good fatty marbling

6 beef short ribs

3 tsp (18 g) salt plus a pinch, divided

¾ tsp freshly ground black pepper, divided

8 tbsp (120 ml) veggie oil, divided

1 large Spanish onion, sliced ⅓ inch (8 mm) thick, divided

8 cloves garlic, minced, divided

1 (15-oz [425-g]) can tomato sauce

1 (15-oz [444-ml]) can low sodium beef broth

2 bay leaves (pinch and crack them for good luck!)

¼ cup (60 ml) soy sauce, plus more to taste

4 large russet or Yukon Gold potatoes, quartered

2 green peppers, cut into bite-sized pieces

¼ tsp red pepper flakes

2 tbsp (32 g) tomato paste

2 cups (400 g) jasmine rice

Let's get this stew brewing. Cut the chuck roast into 2-inch (5-cm) cubes. No need to worry about cutting all the meat around the bone, you'll be cooking that too. If you buy the short ribs that are already packaged into 4-inch (10-cm) cuts, leave it this size. Lightly season both meats with 1 teaspoon of the salt and ½ teaspoon of the pepper.

In a pressure cooker or pot, heat 1 tablespoon (15 ml) of the oil over medium-high heat. I prefer to use a pressure cooker for this dish. Add the meat in batches to sear it, cooking 2 to 3 minutes at a time. Sear in three batches using 1 tablespoon (15 ml) of oil per batch. After it's all browned, place the meat and its juices in a separate bowl and set it aside.

In the emptied pot, heat 1 tablespoon (15 ml) of oil on low heat and sauté half of the sliced onion and 7 of the minced cloves of garlic for 2 to 3 minutes. Be careful not to burn the garlic.

Now return the meat and juices back into the pot. Also add the tomato sauce, beef broth, bay leaves, and soy sauce. Mix and cover. Heat on high until your pressure cooker indicates it's reached its high pressure, then lower the heat and simmer for 20 minutes. If using a regular pot, simmer for 1 hour.

While this cauldron of deliciousness is brewing, place the potatoes in a deep pot filled with cold water that covers them completely. Add 1 teaspoon of the salt and bring to a boil, then lower the heat to simmer for 10 to 15 minutes, or until the potatoes are fork tender. Drain and allow them to continue to steam out, dry and cool for 2 minutes.

While the potatoes are simmering, let's get going on the veggies. In a small sauté pan, heat up 1 tablespoon (15 ml) of oil on medium heat. Add in the other half of the onion, the green peppers, and the remaining clove of garlic. You can't forget the red pepper flakes, ½ teaspoon of salt, and ¼ teaspoon of pepper. Sauté for 5 minutes, then transfer to a serving dish. Clean the pan by simply wiping it out with a paper towel, and keep it handy for use in a bit.

(continued)

TITA KITTY'S *MECHADO* (BEEF 'N' POTATO STEW)
(Continued)

Let's check on our beef. The 20 minutes has come and gone. Go ahead and release the pressure from the cooker gradually. Once the pressure is out, it's safe to open. Fish out the bay leaves with a utensil. Add the tomato paste, and gently mix it into the sauce and beef. This adds a little needed extra flavor, and it helps thicken the sauce too. Cover and set aside.

Using the sauté pan you wiped down, add the remaining 3 tablespoons (45 ml) of oil over medium heat. Spread the oil to coat the pan. Add the potatoes and lightly pan-fry them for 5 to 7 minutes, turning them periodically to brown all sides. Scoop them out and drain them on a paper towel, lightly seasoning with a pinch of salt to taste.

Oh geez, I guess I need to give you steps for Rice 101. One batch of rice for four peeps is about 2 cups (400 g) of uncooked long-grain white rice. Start by getting some of the starchiness out by rinsing and straining it a couple of times. For those of you who own a rice cooker, the ratio of rice to water for this recipe is 2 cups (400 g) of rinsed rice to 2½ cups (600 ml) water.

Stovetop cooking requires additional water. In a small pot or saucepan, combine 3 cups (720 ml) of water and 2 cups (400 g) of rice. Bring to a boil and add the last ½ teaspoon of salt, mix, and cover. Lower the heat and simmer for 15 minutes, or until the water has been absorbed. Turn off the heat and let the rice rest, covered, for 4 minutes. Fork fluff the rice before serving.

To serve, scoop a heaping ladle of beef and sauce over a fluffy bowl of fragrant jasmine rice, and top it off with the sautéed green peppers and onions and your crispy golden fried potatoes. This is exactly how my Momma served it up for me when I was little.

Another delicious way to enjoy *mechado* is to tear off a piece of beautifully crusted bread, slather it with butter, dunk it in the beefy tomato sauce, shovel it up, and munch away.

GRACE'S WINNER–WINNER CHICKEN DINNER

Step right up, come on over, come on in, anybody can play, anybody can win! I've prepared for you a SPECTACULAR meal!

How 'bout it, folks! First up, we've got my CHAMPION CHICKEN!

You've got POTATO CROQUETTES here!

On my RIGHT, a BUTTERY BREAD STUFFING!

To my LEFT, my GROOVY GRAVY that you JUST GOTTA HAVE!

This is a complete chicken dinner roasted to perfection, with a smooth flavor-packed gravy and three delicious sides—a family favorite!

Grab yourself a beer, it's gonna be a fun ride . . . and AWAY we go!

Serves 4

ROAST CHICKEN

5–6 lb (2.3–2.7 kg) chicken, remove giblets and reserve

1 tbsp (18 g) salt

2 tsp (4 g) freshly ground black pepper

KAI'S CROQUETAS (POTATO CROQUETTES)

8 medium Yukon Gold potatoes, cut into small, even chunks

3–4 tbsp (43–58 g) kosher salt, for potato water

4 cloves garlic, minced

1 tbsp (15 ml) olive oil

4 tbsp (56 g) unsalted butter, divided

½ cup (120 ml) heavy cream, warm

3 cups (300 g) of freshly grated Parmesan cheese, divided

4 eggs, whisked

2 cups (112 g) Panko breadcrumbs

2 cups (480 ml) veggie oil

GOTTA HAVE GRAVY

Reserved giblets

3 cups (720 ml) low sodium chicken broth, divided

4 tbsp (56 g) unsalted butter

4 tbsp (31 g) all-purpose flour

¾ cup (180 ml) drippings from roast chicken

BREAD STUFFING

2 sticks (227 g) salted butter

3 white onions, chopped

3 cups (303 g) celery, chopped

3 cups (384 g) carrots, chopped

1 tbsp (2 g) dried sage

1 tsp dried thyme

1 tsp dried marjoram

2 tsp (12 g) salt

½ tsp freshly ground black pepper

1 loaf or 1 lb (450 g) of Italian bread, cut into 2 x 2–inch (5 x 5–cm) cubes (day-old bread preferred)

1 cup (240 ml) low sodium chicken broth

Preparing the stuffing is first on the agenda. It's best to prep this either the day before, my preference, or at least a couple of hours before stuffing the bird. In a large sauté pan, melt the butter on medium heat. Add the onions, celery, carrots, sage, thyme, marjoram, salt, and pepper. Sauté for 5 minutes.

Lay the cubed bread out onto a large baking pan. Pour the melted butter and veggie combo over the bread. Mix to combine well.

Add the chicken broth to the sauté pan and scrape up all the kibbles and bits from the bottom of the pan. This is called deglazing. Then pour this flavorful mix over the bread. Allow stuffing mix to cool, uncovered, for 1 to 2 hours, unless you want to refrigerate it overnight (which I prefer). The stuffing must be cold before putting it into the bird's cavity.

(continued)

～ WINGS! (2 WAYS) ～

I LOVE wings. Wings have to have great flavor and the skins have to be crispy for me to consider them exceptional. For this recipe, I added an Asian twist by marinating my wings, plus I use a 2-fry method to ensure crispiness. I love eating them this way, but like most people, I do also like a bit of heat. Check out my bonus hot sauce recipe if you want to spice things up.

Serves 4

MARINATED WINGS

5 lb (2.3 kg) chicken wings, separate the winglets and drumettes (discard the wing tip portion or pack and freeze it for a future stock)

2 eggs, whisked

2 tbsp (30 ml) soy sauce

1 tsp sesame oil

2 tsp (5 g) garlic powder

1½ tsp (6 g) sugar

1 tsp paprika

½ tsp cayenne pepper

1 tsp salt

½ tsp freshly ground black pepper

2 tbsp (30 ml) Chinese cooking wine or rice wine (see Flip Tip)

1 cup (125 g) all-purpose flour

½ cup (64 g) cornstarch

4 cups (960 ml) veggie oil

LIKE IT HOT (BUTTERY HOT SAUCE)

1 stick (114 g) salted butter

1 tbsp (15 ml) fresh lemon juice

½ cup (120 ml) hot sauce, (I recommend Frank's RedHot)

ACCOMPANIMENTS (CHEF'S CHOICE)

Blue cheese dressing

Ranch dressing

Celery ribs

Carrot sticks

Yellow bell peppers

Mushrooms

In a large bowl, combine the winglets and drumettes with the eggs, soy sauce, sesame oil, garlic powder, sugar, paprika, cayenne pepper, salt, black pepper, and wine. Massage and mix to coat all the chicken pieces, seal the bowl with plastic wrap, and refrigerate for 1½ hours.

Mix the flour and cornstarch in a bowl. Fast forward 1½ hours . . . Take the marinated chicken out of the fridge and strain it. Dredge each piece with the flour and cornstarch mix. Lay the wings out on a baking sheet, and let them sit for 10 to 15 minutes.

I like to deep fry my chicken using a large stock pot. Heat the veggie oil to 325°F (163°C), using your handy oil thermometer to check the temperature. You have approximately 5 pounds (2.3 kg) of chicken here, so it's important to cook it in small batches. I would do five batches, 4 to 5 wings at a time. This way you don't crowd the pot and the correct oil temperature is maintained. Use my 2-fry method, where each batch is initially cooked for 6 minutes, then drained and set on paper towels. This is step 1—the initial fry. Check that the oil temperature is 325°F (163°C), then proceed to step 2—the finish fry. Cook each batch again for 4 more minutes, then drain on paper towels. It's important to continue checking your oil temperature between batches.

When you finish frying, prep my simple hot sauce recipe. Melt the butter in a medium sauce pan. Add the lemon juice and hot sauce. Heat on low for 5 minutes.

Transfer half the chicken into a large mixing bowl, and pour the buttery hot sauce all over it. Mix until each piece is fully coated.

I like to serve the other half of the wings crispy, without sauce. That way you can taste the Asian flair of spices deeply marinated in the juicy wings that you fried to perfection.

Serve with your array of fresh veggies, dressings, and a roll of paper towels. ORDER UP!

FLIP TIP: Shaoxing Wine is a Chinese beverage made from fermented rice that can also be used as a rice wine for cooking. This gives the chicken a traditional Asian flavor. A suitable substitute is *mirin*, a Japanese cooking rice wine, or you can use dry sherry if neither is available.

~ ADOBONG MANOK SA GATA ~
(CHICKEN ADOBO IN COCONUT MILK)

This recipe has literally been passed down and tweaked from generation to generation in my family. It's a fairly simple combo of ingredients, an E-Z dish that packs a ton of flavor. Chicken adobo + coconut milk = *Adobong Manok sa Gata*. Coconut milk, which I call "the magic milk," is the game changer and can be added to many different Filipino dishes, from seafood to pork to veggies. The magic milk transforms traditional Filipino dishes from flavorful to over-the-top DELICIOSO!

Serves 4

1 whole bone-in chicken, cut up, 8 pieces total—2 breasts, 2 thighs, 2 drumsticks, 2 wings

¼ cup (60 ml) white distilled vinegar

¼ cup (60 ml) soy sauce

Pinch of ginger powder

¼ tsp onion powder

½ tsp salt

¼ tsp freshly ground black pepper

2 tbsp (30 g) sugar

1 cup (240 ml) water, divided

7 large cloves garlic, minced

2 tbsp (30 ml) veggie oil

2 (13.5-oz [400-ml]) cans coconut milk

4 pepperoncini peppers, optional

2 tbsp (30 ml) pepperoncini juice, optional

I definitely prepare this a little differently than everyone I know. I like to marinate my chicken the night before, or at least 4 hours before it hits the pan. So a morning marination for a lunch or dinner meal would work.

Take the cut-up chicken and place it into a sealer bag, along with the vinegar, soy sauce, ginger powder, onion powder, salt, pepper, sugar, ½ cup (120 ml) of the water, and the garlic. Shake the bag and refrigerate overnight, or at least 4 hours.

Now that the chicken is marinated, use tongs to transfer the chicken to a paper towel-lined plate, and pat it dry. Discard the marinade in the bag.

In a large nonstick pan over medium heat, add the veggie oil and spread it all over the surface of the pan. Quickly brown the chicken on both sides, about 5 minutes total. Lower the heat and pour in ½ cup (120 ml) of water. Add the coconut milk, pepperoncini peppers and pepperoncini juice, if using, and simmer over low heat for an additional 20 minutes.

The sauce should appear thickened after this time has passed. If the sauce is too watery, remove the chicken from the pan and place it in a covered serving dish to keep it warm. Increase the heat to medium and simmer for another 10 minutes, or until the sauce thickens, then pour it back over the chicken.

That's it folks, there you have it. Chicken smothered in a rich coconut sauce with a touch of heat. For an added bit of sweet heat, offer up a side of pepperoncinis. I like serving this with a traditional Filipino veggie combo of green beans sautéed with tomatoes, onions, and garlic. And, of course, you always have the option to serve it over rice!

GRILLED *CARNE ASADA*
(SKIRT STEAK)

I like to grill outdoors as much as the next guy. No matter what the weather forecast, I always find a way to get my grill on. Years ago, I was invited to a Carne Asada—yup, you read that right, a Carne Asada. It's very similar to an American barbecue, and it was absolutely the coolest display I've ever seen. All walks of people taking pride in their own live fire-making techniques, using both firepits and grills, showcasing prize-winning family recipes, yielding the tastiest feast.

I grew up eating a dish called *carne asada*. It's a beautifully charred grilled beef infused with oils, spices, and calamansi, a Philippine lime. I created this recipe to pay homage to all the grill masters of the world, whose passion for cooking is unmatched by their drive to find that perfect fire.

Serves 4

MARINADE

½ cup (8 g) fresh cilantro, or substitute a mix of dill and parsley

½ tsp salt

½ tsp freshly ground black pepper

½ cup (120 ml) olive oil

1 tsp lemon zest

1 tsp lime zest

2 tbsp (30 ml) lemon juice, freshly squeezed

2 tbsp (30 ml) lime juice, freshly squeezed

¼ cup (55 g) light brown sugar

¼ cup (60 ml) soy sauce

SKIRT STEAK

2 lb (900 g) skirt steak

10 flour tortillas

2 tbsp (30 ml) veggie oil

Pinch of red pepper flakes

1 large Spanish onion, sliced

2 tbsp (17 g) garlic, minced

1 tbsp (14 g) salted butter

4 portobello mushrooms, sliced thinly

TOPPERS

1 lemon, wedged

1 lime, wedged

Mexican Cotija, Queso Fresco, or your favorite cheese, shredded

Hot sauce

Sour cream

For the marinade, combine the cilantro, salt, pepper, oil, lemon zest, lime zest, lemon juice, lime juice, sugar, and soy sauce. Before you add your meat, reserve 2 tablespoons (30 ml) of the marinade for an onion and mushroom sauté. Marinate the skirt steak in a large sealer bag for at least 1 to 4 hours. I suggest you let it go up to the 4-hour mark—the longer you marinate, the tastier it will be.

Here's a bonus suggestion for ya. If you like salsa, a little bit of guacamole or both, check out the recipes in my Homie Chips 'n' Pico de Guaco (page 26). It's a good time to whip them up while the meat is marinating.

Once the steak is marinated, get your grill piping hot. Grill the marinated skirt steak for 5 to 6 minutes per side, depending on the thickness of the cut. Let it rest for 5 minutes. Why do we let the meat rest? It's simply to allow the juices to redistribute through the meat. If you cut it immediately after it's taken off the heat, the juices will run right out and you'll end up with a dry slab of yuck.

While the meat is resting, heat a sauté pan over medium heat. In the dry pan, place a fresh white flour tortilla, and heat through for 30 to 40 seconds on each side. Repeat this process with the rest and put the warmed tortillas on a plate, covering them with a clean kitchen towel.

Let's use the same pan and heat up the oil. Toss in the red pepper flakes, then the onion, garlic, butter, mushrooms, and 2 tablespoons (30 ml) of reserved marinade. Sauté for 10 minutes over medium-high heat.

Don't you worry, I'm not neglecting the tender and juicy steak, chillax. Slice the steak against the grain, which means cutting through fibers instead of along the direction they run. This makes the meat easier to chew.

OK, on to the fajita party. Grab your warm tortilla, fork up a helping of carne asada, scoop in some shrooms, add a squeeze of citrus, top with cheese, hot sauce, and sour cream. *Salud!*

～ TERIYUMMI BEEF ～

Beef teriyaki is one of my favorite meals. It's all about the sweet, gingery soy sauce mix that makes my taste buds say THANK YOU! Kids of all ages seem to like this dish, and parents like it 'cause they can sneak a bunch of veggies in that aren't just covered with cheese. It's not "YAKI" to me, it's one big plate of "YUMMI."

Serves 4

BEEF AND VEGGIES

2 cups (400 g) long grain white rice, rinsed (see Flip Tip)

3½ tsp (21 g) salt, divided, plus more to taste

2 cups (182 g) broccoli florets

1½ lb (680 g) sirloin steak, sliced ⅛ inch (3 mm) thick (freeze the meat for about an hour first for easier slicing)

¼ tsp pepper, plus more to taste

6 tbsp (90 ml) veggie oil, divided

2 cloves garlic, chopped, divided

Pinch of red pepper flakes

1 medium Spanish onion, sliced

1 cup (70 g) mushrooms, sliced (buttons or bellas are great)

1 red bell pepper, sliced

3 green onions, sliced, divided (white bottoms for sauté, green tops for garnish)

1 (8-oz [227-g]) can water chestnuts, drained, sliced

SAUCE

2 tbsp (16 g) cornstarch

2 tbsp (30 ml) water

¼ cup (60 ml) soy sauce

½ cup (120 ml) low sodium beef broth

¼ cup (55 g) brown sugar

1 tsp ginger, minced

1 clove garlic, minced

1 tbsp (15 ml) honey

1 tsp sesame oil

TOPPERS

Green onion tops, reserved

1 cup (146 g) cashew nuts, toasted, optional

¼ cup (36 g) sesame seeds, toasted, optional

Rice 101: For those of you who own a rice cooker, the ratio of rice to water for this recipe is 2 cups (400 g) of rinsed rice to 2½ cups (600 ml) of water. Stovetop cooking requires additional water. In a small pot or saucepan, combine 3 cups (720 ml) of water and the rice. Bring to a boil and add ½ teaspoon of salt, mix, and cover. Lower the heat and simmer for 15 minutes. Turn off the heat and let the rice rest, covered, for 4 minutes. Fork fluff the rice before serving.

For the sauce, start by mixing the cornstarch and water into a thickening slurry, then set aside. Combine the soy sauce, beef broth, brown sugar, ginger, garlic, honey, and sesame oil in a small sauce pan. Heat to boiling, then simmer for 5 minutes. Add the slurry to the sauce, and heat it for a couple more minutes until the sauce thickens. So far the rice and the sauce are on deck.

Broccoli florets need to be blanched before beef comes into the picture. This is done to retain their color, flavor, texture, and nutrition. So bring a pot of water to a boil and add the remaining 3 teaspoons (17 g) of salt. Drop in the florets and let them cook for 3 to 4 minutes. Prep a bowl of ice water while the broccoli is blanching. Scoop out the broccoli and fully submerge them in the bowl of ice water to shock them and to stop the cooking process. Allow them to cool for 2 minutes. Once cooled, scoop them out, and set it aside 'til the other veggies are up to bat.

Season the meat with salt and pepper right before you cook it. Heat a nonstick pan—or a wok, to get the whole Asian vibe going—over high heat. Add 2 tablespoons (30 ml) of the veggie oil and 1 clove of the chopped garlic. Place half of the meat in the pan, and sear it for a quick 3 to 4 minutes. Scoop it out, set it aside, and repeat the process with 2 more tablespoons (30 ml) of oil, the remaining clove of garlic, and the remaining beef. Set aside and cover.

Veggie time, folks. Turn the heat to medium-high, and add 2 more tablespoons (30 ml) of oil to your pan. Then in go the red pepper flakes, onion, shrooms, bell pepper, green onion bottoms, water chestnuts, and the blanched broccoli. Give them a dash of salt and pepper, and sauté for 5 minutes.

Invite the beef back to the party! Pour in the sauce, and thoroughly toss it all together. Top with your sliced green onion tops. To jazz it up, top with toasted cashews and sesame seeds. Serve with white rice!

FLIP TIP: When cooking rice, use chicken or veggie broth instead of water and salt for more flavor.

⌁ ADOBO-WAN KENOBI ⌁
(BRAISED PORK)

A long time ago, in my Lola's kitchen far, far away . . . a traditional Filipino pork dish, *Adobong Baboy* was made. Hyperdrive to my present-day kitchen where I once again Americanized a Filipino dish a bit. This time I've applied a flavorful searing technique, and added apple cider vinegar and beer to my special braising brew. The main ingredients of Filipino *Adobo* are white vinegar, soy sauce, black peppercorns, and bay leaves. I've included pork belly and additional aromatics to my braising liquid to give it a boost and more depth of flavor. For even more flavor and texture, those bellies are fried to a crisp! Hopefully, my Lola will approve of my tweaks. I can already feel her pinching my cheeks.

Serves 4

1½ lb (680 g) pork shoulder

2 tbsp (16 g) flour

2 tbsp (16 g) cornstarch

1 tbsp (8 g) garlic powder

½ tsp salt

¼ tsp freshly ground black pepper

3 tbsp (45 ml) plus ¼ cup (60 ml) veggie oil, divided

½ cup (60 ml) soy sauce

¼ cup (60 ml) white distilled vinegar

¼ cup (60 ml) apple cider vinegar

1 cup (240 ml) of cold water

1 large onion, sliced

7 whole black peppercorns

7 cloves garlic, divided, 4 smashed for braising, 3 minced

2 bay leaves (pinch and crack them for good luck!)

½ cup (120 ml) beer, optional

½ lb (227 g) slab of pork belly

¼ tsp fish sauce (*patis*), optional

I use both pork belly and pork shoulder in this dish. Why? 'Cause the double whammy of fat content in these cuts will yield an amazing flavor.

Cut up the pork shoulder into 1 x 2–inch (2.5 x 5–cm) pieces. The butcher will happily do this for you upon request. Mix the flour, cornstarch, and garlic powder in a small bowl. Salt and pepper each piece of pork, and lightly dust it with a coating of the flour, cornstarch, and garlic powder mix. Save the mix for later.

Now we're going to sear the pork shoulder in three batches. For each batch, coat the bottom of a stock pot with 1 tablespoon (15 ml) of oil over high heat. Sear the pork shoulder for 1 to 2 minutes on each side. Repeat twice.

In a bowl, combine the soy sauce, white vinegar, apple cider vinegar, water, onion, peppercorns, 4 smashed cloves of garlic, bay leaves, and beer if you're using it.

Place the pork belly and the seared pork shoulder pieces back into the stock pot. Add the soy sauce mixture and bring to a boil. Cover and simmer for 1 hour and 15 minutes, until the meat is fork tender.

Carefully scoop out all the meat with a slotted spoon. Strain the broth from the pot, then pour the broth back into the pot to simmer and reduce for 15 minutes.

Pork belly holds up to the braising process and will not fall apart. This meat with its high fat content must first be boiled or braised in order for it to fry properly. Take the pork belly and slice it into 1-inch (2.5-cm) pieces. Dry with paper towels by pressing down to absorb as much moisture as possible.

Fully dredge the pork belly in the flour, cornstarch and garlic powder coating mix made earlier. This mix helps with crisping and reduces the liquid splattering of moist meat. This is a cheat to mimic the traditional drying method of *Lechon Kawali*, a Filipino dish of crispy, pan-fried pork belly that you would otherwise have to dry for a few hours to a full day before frying.

(continued)

ADOBO-WAN KENOBI (BRAISED PORK)
(Continued)

Grab a separate sauté pan and heat the remaining ¼ cup (60 ml) of oil. Fry the coated pork belly slices 'til they're crispy, about 3 to 4 minutes on each side. Careful, the oil does splatter. Holy smokes, folks, it is SO good, talk about an over-the-top treat!

White rice and any type of veggies go well with this dish. I like to "get my flip on" with a traditional cold medley of fresh veggies: chopped tomatoes, steamed green beans and sliced white onions topped with quartered hard-boiled eggs and seasoned with salt and pepper and a splash or two of fish sauce. The melding of braised meats in with the natural juices and oils they render produce a sinfully succulent balance of tender meats immersed in a rich, hearty stew. Pour it over everything—Have MERCY!

～ I SPY A RIBEYE ～
(INCLUDES BAKED POTATO)

A steak, a baked potato, and a helping of buttery garlic corn is my go-to combo for a perfect meal. I'M SOLD. This dinner ranks in the top 10 most belly-satisfying meals ever in my book. Seriously, a ribeye steak meal instantly pops into my head when I want to treat myself after a good day, a bad day, or just to MAKE MY DAY. Whip this up with Gimme Garlic Corn (page 42) to make yours!

Serves 2

RIB EYE

2 (1¼-inch [3-cm]) bone-in ribeye steaks, room temp

1 tbsp (18 g) kosher salt

1½ tsp freshly ground black pepper

2 tbsp (30 ml) olive oil

6 cloves of garlic, crushed

2–3 sprigs of fresh rosemary

2–3 sprigs of fresh thyme

½ stick (56 g) salted butter

2 tbsp (30 ml) soy sauce, optional

BAKED TATERS

2–4 medium to large russet potatoes

½ stick (56 g) salted butter, room temp

1 tbsp (18 g) salt, plus more to taste

½ tsp freshly ground black pepper

So what do you need to make this happen? Start with window shopping at your butcher or the meat section of your grocery store, and be on the lookout for a ribeye steak. Butchers are always happy to help, and can cut a ribeye for you. I use a 1¼-inch (3-cm) thickness, but remember the thicker it is, the longer it takes to cook.

Preheat the oven to 450°F (232°C). Let's start with the potatoes: wash and scrub them under cold water, then poke them all over with a fork, about ½ inch (1.3 cm) deep. Place them onto a baking sheet and bake for 23 minutes. The skins should look aged, dry, and wrinkly when they're done.

Take the pan out of the oven, flip the potatoes, and give them a good slather of butter all over. It's E-Z to do this using room temperature butter and a basting brush. The butter immediately melts when it hits the hot potato skins. Rain on a good amount of salt on all sides, and place them back into the oven for another 23 minutes of baking.

While the potatoes finish baking, hop over to my Gimme Garlic Corn (page 42) recipe for the perfect veggie side!

Let's get our steaks on. First, pat the steaks dry and then liberally, yes, liberally season them with salt and freshly ground pepper. When I cook a steak, I typically like to use a cast iron pan. Heat the pan over medium-high heat before you add the steak; the idea is to have a hot pan to get the desired char on the steak. FYI, you will be creating a bit of smoke, so vents and a window should be open. Not kidding. Add in the oil and heat 'til you see a ripple, but no smoke. Carefully place the steak in the pan.

(continued)

I SPY A RIBEYE (INCLUDES BAKED POTATO)
(Continued)

Place the garlic and sprigs of rosemary and thyme onto the open area of the hot pan. Dollop in the butter and allow the steak to sear for 5 minutes to create a beautiful, crusty char. Flip the steak. Next step is to start basting the meat with spoonfuls of the buttery, aromatic olive oil mix. It's best to tilt the handle of the skillet down towards you slightly, so the oil gathers to make it easier to spoon up.

If you like medium-rare steak like I do, cook for 3 to 4 minutes. Continue to baste about 3 to 4 times during this cooking process. To check the desired doneness, use a meat thermometer. I pull my steak off the heat when it hits 120°F (49°C) and place it on a cutting board. For a medium-rare steak, you want an internal temperature of 125°F (52°C), and it will continue to cook while on the board. Let the steak rest for 5 to 7 minutes to allow the juices to redistribute and settle throughout the ribeye.

I slice the meat relatively thin, so I try to make ⅛-inch (3-mm) slices against the grain and on the bias, which makes for a tender and not chewy bite. Get your potatoes and cut them in half. Then season with salt and pepper, and top with butter or sour cream.

To make a yummy steak sauce, allow the pan to cool for a few minutes. Discard the garlic and thyme sprigs. Add in the soy sauce, mix, and serve on top of the steak or as a dipping sauce on the side. Serve the steak alongside the taters and corn.

Oh man you guys, my mouth is watering up a storm. Have a great meal and CHEERS TO YOU!

STEAK TEMPERATURE CHEAT SHEET

Rare: 115°F (46°C)

Medium-rare: 125°F (49°C)

Medium-well: 135°F (57°C)

Overcooked (well-done): 150°F (66°C)

Seafood, Time to Swim!

As much as I like a bit of "turf," I cannot deny my craving for "surf." Thankfully, I was introduced to seafood at an early age, and I was taught to never swim away from an opportunity to taste a new variety of fish. I discovered that I like them all!

I've got some tasty seafood recipes for you in this chapter. You can relax from a tough day with an E-Z fish pouch, or kick it up a nautical notch with a paella when you're ready to party. These recipes are family favorites and all quite deliciously doable. Please don't shy away from trying out a shellfish dish like my 3 Shell Soup (page 88). When you're already in deep, you might as well test the waters of your taste buds and dive into some shrimp, like my Tempting Tempura (page 84).

I have complete faith in you. Take a deep breath and plunge confidently into your cooking skills. Soon enough, you'll be floating by on the knowledge that YOU created a delicious seafood meal, no S.O.S needed!

~ LOVELY JUBBLY FISH 'N' CHIPS ~

I can already taste the crisp crunch of this beer-battered fish. I have visions of me dousing each bite with malt vinegar and dipping my fish in cocktail sauce. Lucky me, or perhaps lucky you, I already have a good French fry recipe, Fresh Fries Please, I'll Wait! (page 41) for the "chips" portion of this meal. Just remember to prep and cook the fries before you dredge, dunk, and dip the fish, and while you're at it, try my Fools 'n' Sauces (page 160) for dipping!

Serves 4

4 cups (960 ml) veggie oil

2 lb (900 g) skinless haddock filets (cod and pollock are great substitutes, but the cut of fish is important—it should be a filet, and not a steak, folks)

1 tsp Old Bay seasoning

2 cups (250 g) all-purpose flour, divided

⅓ cup (43 g) cornstarch

½ tsp salt

¼ tsp freshly ground black pepper

1 tbsp (14 g) baking powder

1 tsp garlic powder

1 tsp onion powder

1 (12-oz [355-ml]) bottle COLD beer (lager or ale), or club soda for non-alcoholic option

Malt vinegar or pickled onions, to serve, optional

Preheat the oven to 250°F (121°C) and start heating up the oil in a deep pot. Each batch of fish will be placed on a baking sheet in the oven to keep it warm while you're frying the other batches, as well as when you're finishing off the fries.

First, let's prep the fries so we can properly time them to be served hot. This means to just semi-cook them for now. Follow my Fresh Fries Please, I'll Wait! (page 41) instructions: parboil, cut, coat, and fry for only 3 minutes. Drain, but DO NOT SALT. I use the same pot of oil to cook both the fish and fries, but if you want a separate pot for fries so they won't taste fishy, go for it. Set aside 'til we finish frying the fish.

Pat the filets dry of any excess moisture, and ya might as well have extra paper towels handy to drain the fish. Set yourself up with two separate containers—one for flour mix dredging and the other for cold beer batter dunking. The dredge is a mix of the Old Bay and ½ cup (63 g) of the flour. The batter is a mix of 1½ cups (188 g) of the flour plus the cornstarch, salt and pepper, baking powder, garlic powder, onion powder, and 1 COLD bottle of beer. Combine and mix well. Have I mentioned the beer should be cold? The coldness and carbonation of the beer helps the batter fry up light and crisp.

Check on your oil using a thermometer, to make sure it's reached 375°F (190°C).

Prepare to get your hands a little messy here. Lightly dredge the fish in the flour mix and pat off the excess. Dunk the fish into the batter, which will stick to the flour dredge. Whatever drips off, let it drip off. It's best to fry two portions at a time to help maintain the oil temperature. Carefully place the battered fish into the oil, laying it down away from you to avoid splatter. I use my hands 'cause I'm used to it, but tongs will help you avoid most of the splatter.

(continued)

LOVELY JUBBLY FISH 'N' CHIPS (Continued)

Fry for 5 minutes, until the batter turns to a light golden brown, turning the filets over once. Use a slotted spoon to scoop them out of the oil, and drain the filets on paper towels. Then place them onto the baking sheet in the warming oven. Repeat for the remaining batches.

Back to the fries. Check that the oil temperature is still 375°F (190°C). Finish frying the fries in four batches. Remember, you already cooked them halfway, so it will be another quick 3 minutes per batch. Keep the batches warm in the oven with the fish while you finish off cooking all the fries. You're doing an amazing job juggling the timing!

Serve the fish and chips with malt vinegar. Maybe even give pickled onions a go, you won't regret it!

~ KINDA CALI ROLLS ~

I definitely am an "I could eat sushi every week" person. It's mesmerizing to watch skilled sushi chefs create little works of edible art, and having a front seat to such talented crafters through the years has helped me muster the courage to give it a go. As it turns out, you don't need to be a Jedi Master to make sushi. All you need are two things: First, a good sushi rice recipe. Hello, that's why I'm here. Second, your creativity switch needs be turned on.

I like to make an American version of *Uramaki*, rolls where the rice is on the outside. Here, I've created a LO-version of a California roll. Serve with my One-Two Ponzu sauce (page 155)!

Yields 6 rolls

2 cups (400 g) sushi rice	½ cup (72 g) sesame seeds, toasted in a dry pan on low heat for two minutes
¼ cup (60 ml) rice wine vinegar	
1 tsp sugar	½ cup (72 g) black sesame seeds, optional
1 tsp salt	
½ lb (227 g) lump crabmeat	1 medium carrot, julienned
	½ cucumber, seeded, julienned
3 tbsp (45 ml) mayo	
1 tbsp (15 ml) sriracha	1 ripe avocado, optional
1 tsp oyster sauce	Wasabi paste, to serve, optional
1 package Nori seaweed sheets, cut in half lengthwise	Pickled ginger, to serve, optional

OK, so let's talk rice. A rice cooker is the best way to cook rice every day. You'll need 2 cups (400 g) of sushi rice, which is usually a short grain glutenous rice. Thankfully, sushi is so popular in the U.S. that many rice producers have made a variety of grocery brands marked conveniently "sushi rice."

Rinse and drain the rice a couple of times in order to take out as much starch as possible. When cooking rice in a rice cooker, use 2½ cups (600 ml) of water. Prep a combo of the rice vinegar, sugar, and salt, mixing until the sugar is dissolved. Once the rice is cooked, pour the mixture over the rice and fluff.

WHAT, no rice cooker? I gotcha, no worries, stove top cooking works just as well. In a heavy pot, pour in 2 cups (400 g) of rinsed and drained sushi rice. Add 3 cups (720 ml) water, bring to a boil, then reduce heat to low and simmer for 20 minutes. Prep the combo of the rice vinegar, sugar, and salt, mixing until the sugar is dissolved. After it's cooked, pour over the rice and fluff. Déjà vu, haha.

Alrighty now, let's get to some fun sushi filling. Combine the lump crabmeat, mayo, sriracha, and oyster sauce in a bowl and set it aside. If you want a crunchy Cali roll, wrap up some Tempting Tempura (page 84).

Ahhh, the ROLLING OF THE ROLL . . . I can't do this without a bamboo mat that's entirely wrapped in plastic wrap. Place half a sheet of nori on the mat, with the rough side up to grip the rice. Spread ⅓ cup (67 g) of sushi rice onto the nori, pressing it down and leaving a ½-inch (1.3-cm) lip without rice along the edge farthest away from you. Make it a thin coat and not a solid wall, otherwise it will roll up wayyyy too thick, which is a common mistake. Sprinkle toasted and/or black sesame seeds onto the rice throughout, then flip the nori over, still keeping the lip without the rice farthest away from you.

The plain shiny side of the nori is now facing up. Starting about 1 inch (2.5 cm) from the edge closest to you, dollop the crab spread from the left edge of the nori, working your way to the right edge. This should be about 5 teaspoons (25 g) of the crab mix. Place a few sticks of carrots on top of the crab, again from left to right, distributing them evenly. Repeat this step with the cucumber.

(continued)

KINDA CALI ROLLS (Continued)

Carefully pick up the edge of the nori closest to you to start a tight roll. Using the mat and both hands to help fold over the roll, roll away from yourself. Firmly roll and press down, but don't squeeze too hard or else the crab filling will squirt out of both ends.

Is it safe to say you've had success? I hope so, but remember, practice makes perfect! I do like to add a fanned avocado on top before I slice the roll. I simply cut a ripe avocado in half, take out the seed, then peel the skin off. Slice each half thinly while keeping its shape. Gently push down, fanning out the avocado to fit the length of the roll. Now slide a knife underneath and carefully transfer it on top of the roll. Place a sheet of plastic wrap over the avocado-topped roll. Gently form the avocado onto the roll through the wrap. Use a super sharp knife and slice it into 8 pieces, or cut it in half for a larger serving.

Dip your sushi into my One-Two Ponzu (page 155) for a tasty, citrusy soy with a side of wasabi and pickled ginger. THAT'S HOW I ROLL!

Crispy shrimp tempura is truly a temptation for me. Why? It's so ridiculously E-Z to prepare. Plans of making this as an appetizer for myself always change, and it becomes the main meal. Temptation wins most days. It's great to serve at parties, and is always the first to go. I get a kick out of the sight of people restraining themselves from grabbing more than just a couple at a time. I recognize a shrimp fiend when I see one, it makes me chuckle. People say they just can't get enough of it and ask me if the secret is in the batter or the marinade. Tempt yourself, and you tell me! Try my Lucky Ducky Sauce (page 152) and One-Two Ponzu (page 155) for dipping.

Serves 4

1 lb (454 g) jumbo shrimp, 21–25 count, shell and tail on

½ cup (120 ml) white vinegar or rice wine vinegar

1 tsp salt, divided

8 peppercorns, crushed (if you only have regular pepper, use ¼ tsp)

7 cloves garlic, minced

¼ cup (60 ml) water

1 cup (125 g) all-purpose flour

3 tbsp (24 g) cornstarch

1 tsp baking powder

¼ tsp white pepper (black is OK too)

1 tbsp (7 g) paprika, optional

1 egg

⅔ cup (160 ml) fizzy liquid, SUPER COLD club soda or beer (just not a dark beer)

4 cups (960 ml) veggie oil

Cooking time is fairly short, just a few minutes frying in small batches until you've reached that recognizable golden-brown goodness. Let's get into it and prep the shrimp and marinade. I don't mess around here, folks—I use jumbo shrimp. De-shell, leaving the tail on, devein, and rinse to clean. I leave the tail on 'cause it's a cool handle, and it looks fancy.

Combine the vinegar, ½ teaspoon salt, crushed peppercorns, garlic, and water. Submerge the shrimp into this vinegar combo mix, cover, and set aside to marinate for 20 minutes.

The batter preparation is just as simple. It's best to wait until the shrimp is fully marinated to mix it. In a large bowl, thoroughly combine the flour, cornstarch, baking powder, remaining ½ teaspoon of salt, white pepper, and paprika (if using) before adding in the egg and your super cold fizzy liquid. Smooth out the batter as much as possible, but small lumps are fine, no worries.

Now I wish I had a deep fryer, but sadly my birthday is a few months away so I use what's available. If you don't have one either, choose a deep pot for frying. Make sure it's deep enough to hold the veggie oil and keep you protected from any spattering. Use a high heat to bring the temperature of the oil up to 375°F (190°C), and make sure to test it with an oil thermometer. You can also do a fry test by dropping a little batter into the oil. If the batter begins to sizzle and bubble up, then you'll know the oil is getting hot.

Working in small batches when frying anything is always the way to go. Dip the shrimp in the batter one at a time, and fry them. A fry time of 3 to 4 minutes should be sufficient. Small-batch frying helps keep the oil at the optimum temperature. It also helps you to not get too overwhelmed monitoring a high number of shrimp, which can lead them to burn. Scoop up the golden-brown shrimp with a mesh strainer-scooper, as I call it, and drain on a bunch of paper towels.

Obviously, these shrimp are best served immediately. Don't forget to use my special dipping sauces. Do you think you can wait to eat one before the rest of the family comes down for dinner? Go on, give in—you know you wanna.

～ OH BOY, PO' BOY! ～

Oh wow, a fried shrimp po' boy! This sandwich brings back mad fun memories of good times in New Orleans. My first taste was at a jazz festival back in the '90s. I asked one of the service vendors why my sandwich was called a po' boy, and to my geeky delight, she provided me with a history lesson. Back in the day, striking street car workers were known as "poor boys," which in Louisiana slang is pronounced "po' boys." The workers were served free sandwiches as a peace offering, in an attempt calm them down during the difficult multi-month-long strike. I've heard many other variations of the story, but this is the one that stuck with me.

Fun Fact: There are also many different versions of this New Orleans street food. Fried oyster po' boys are quite popular, while some other po' boys have no seafood at all. I'm sure each version is delicious, but my heart and taste buds always lead me back to my love at first bite: the shrimp po' boy. Prep Lady Remoulade (page 167) or Aioli Moli (page 164) before you cook!

Serves 4

PO' MARINADE

½ cup (120 ml) white vinegar or rice wine vinegar

½ tsp salt

8 peppercorns, crushed (if you only have regular pepper, use ¼ tsp)

7 cloves garlic, minced

¼ cup (60 ml) water

1 tbsp (15 ml) hot sauce, (I recommend Frank's RedHot)

1 lb (454 g) jumbo shrimp, 21–25 count, shells and tails removed

PO' BATTER

1 cup (125 g) all-purpose flour

3 tbsp (24 g) cornstarch

1 tsp baking powder

½ tsp salt plus a pinch, divided

¼ tsp white pepper (black is OK too)

1 tbsp (7 g) paprika, optional

½ tsp cayenne pepper

¼ tsp dried oregano

¼ tsp dried thyme

1 egg

⅔ cup (160 ml) fizzy liquid, SUPER COLD club soda or beer (just not a dark beer)

SANDWICH FIXINGS

4 cups (960 ml) veggie oil

4 (10-inch [25-cm]) French rolls or baguettes, buttered, lightly toasted

Shredded lettuce

Sliced tomatoes

Pinch of pepper

To make the marinade, combine the vinegar, salt, peppercorns, garlic, water, and hot sauce in a bowl. Submerge the shrimp into this vinegar combo mix, cover, and set it aside to marinate for 20 minutes.

The batter preparation is just as simple, but it's best to wait until the shrimp is fully marinated to make it. In a large bowl, thoroughly combine the flour, cornstarch, baking powder, ½ teaspoon salt, pepper, paprika (if using), cayenne, oregano, and thyme before adding in the egg and your super cold fizzy liquid. Smooth out the batter as much as possible, but small lumps are fine.

Add the oil into a deep pot and heat to 375°F (190°C). You can do a fry test by dropping a little batter into the oil. If the batter begins to sizzle and bubble up, then you'll know the oil is getting hot.

Frying in batches is always the best way to go. Dip a small batch of shrimp into the batter, one at a time, and transfer them to the oil. A fry time of 3 to 4 minutes should be sufficient. Scoop up the golden-brown shrimp with a mesh strainer-scooper, as I call it, and drain them on a bunch of paper towels.

Finally, take your bread and smear on one of the creamy sauces (page 167 or page 164). Arrange a bed of crisp, shredded lettuce on a roll, and then a layer of perfectly ripe tomatoes. Season with a pinch of salt and pepper. Now top this off with a mound, yes a mound, of crispy fried shrimp. Seal the deal with the other half of the toasted roll and DIVE IN!

⏤ 3 SHELL SOUP ⏤

Yowza, this recipe brings back some seriously fond memories. I ate a version of this soup every other day when I used to live and work in Ocean City, Maryland. The heart of this soup is a Maryland She-Crab, but I've added some other seafood and spices to create my take on that delicious soup. We've gone from a hit-the-spot East Coast rave to an over-the-top homemade fave. This soup's spicy blend of tomato, vegetable, and seafood flavors should make the top of your bucket list of food to try.

Serves 4 to 8

1 lb (454 g) mussels, 20–25 count

12 cherry or little neck clams

¼ cup (32 g) kosher salt

2 tbsp (30 ml) olive oil

Pinch of red pepper flakes

1 cup (128 g) carrots, sliced or cubed

1 medium onion, diced

2 cloves garlic, minced

1 medium red potato, peeled, cubed

2 ribs of celery, trimmed, sliced thinly

1 cup (136 g) corn, frozen, or 2 ears of fresh, cut from the cob

½ cup (80 g) lima beans, fresh or frozen

1 cup (110 g) green beans, fresh or frozen

3 cups (720 ml) of water

2 cups (480 ml) low sodium beef stock

1 tbsp (15 ml) Worcestershire sauce

1 tbsp (15 ml) fresh lemon juice

1 tbsp (8 g) Old Bay seasoning

Pinch of dried thyme

1 (28-oz [794-g]) can peeled whole tomatoes, undrained

1 lb (454 g) crabmeat, preferably lump, but claw is fine

Salt and pepper, to taste

Oyster crackers or cheddar Goldfish crackers, to serve

Before scrubbing the mussels and clams, submerge them for 15 minutes in cold water that's been salted with the kosher salt. This will help the sea creatures to expel sand and grit from inside their shells, and will help them release their grip on the anchored beard. Then you can scrub and debeard them.

Let's shove off! Heat up the olive oil in a large pot or Dutch oven, over medium heat. Add in the red pepper flakes, carrots, onion, garlic, potato, celery, corn, lima beans, and green beans. Sauté for 10 minutes. Pour in the water, beef stock, Worcestershire sauce, and lemon juice, then add the Old Bay seasoning and thyme. Next is the tomatoes, but I like to crush the tomatoes in my hand first before adding them. Oh, and yes, pour in the juice from the can too. Bring this cauldron of deliciousness to a boil over medium-high heat, then reduce heat to medium-low and simmer for 25 minutes.

Add the crabmeat, mussels, and clams to the soup, then simmer 10 minutes more. Stir often but gently, please. Season to taste with salt and pepper. That's it!

Serve with oyster crackers, or, I kid you not, cheddar Goldfish crackers!

E-Z PEASY SEAFOOD POUCH
(BAKED COD)

I made this on the spot for my Pop one day, 'cause he was eating way too much red meat and I wanted to show him a heart-healthy meal that's quick, E-Z and delicious! I knew I wanted to stay away from frying, I needed a fish that would hold up to the baking process, and that it was a must to include as many fresh veggies as possible. I also wanted to make sure I used some common Filipino aromatics that his taste buds would recognize, like ginger, garlic, onion, and tomatoes, to create a nice vegetable combo called *ginisá*. This is the Filipino base for flavoring stocks, sauces, and other foods. The empty pouch said it all; he loved it! I'm sure you will too. It looks fancy, but it's an E-Z prep meal with E-Z clean-up that's simple enough for a family dinner and delicious enough for company.

Yields 1 pouch

1 (6-oz [170-g]) cod filet	3 cremini or button mushrooms, sliced
Pinch of salt	½-inch (1.2-cm) nub of fresh ginger, grated or ¼ tsp ginger powder
Pinch of pepper	
⅛ tsp dried thyme	1 clove garlic, minced
⅛ tsp dried mustard	2 lemon wedges, divided
¼ tsp paprika, sweet or smokey	1 small handful of baby spinach
1 splash of hot sesame oil	1 tbsp (14 g) salted butter
1 tsp olive oil	1 green onion, chopped
¼ Spanish onion, sliced	¼ cup (60 ml) vegetable broth
6 grape tomatoes, whole	
½ rib celery, cut on the bias	

What's great about this recipe is you don't have to wait until the fish is thawed to start cooking it. Cod, like haddock, is a great fish to work with when making any fish entrée. It's thicker and firmer than most, so it's not going to overcook easily the way a thinner fish, like tilapia, would.

Preheat the oven to 375°F (190°C).

Get a sheet of foil the length of your arm, then fold it in half to make a stronger double sheet. Grab a soup bowl, then push the aluminum sheet into the center to mold it, forming an aluminum bowl. Leave it in the bowl to keep everything steady as you assemble the pouch with all the ingredients.

If your fish is thawed, let's season it with the salt, pepper, thyme, mustard, paprika, and sesame oil. No need to do this step if it's frozen, because nothing will stick to a frozen filet. If your filet is frozen, save the seasoning.

Coat the pouch-like bowl with the olive oil. Next, place the sliced onion at the bottom, and layer the tomatoes, celery and mushrooms on top. Sprinkle in the ginger and garlic.

Place the cod filet on top of the veggies, and if your filet is frozen now is when you'll add the salt, pepper, thyme, mustard, paprika, and sesame oil. Squeeze one lemon wedge over the fish. Throw in your baby spinach, butter, and green onion. Top off your seafood sensation with the veggie broth.

You are ready to seal up the pouch! I basically fold up the aluminum foil while it's still in the bowl, sheet to sheet. I start twisting the edges together at one end, from left to right. It's like I'm sealing the edges of a calzone. Then lift the pouch out of the bowl and onto a baking sheet. Bake on the center rack for 20 minutes if the filet was thawed, 25 minutes if it was frozen.

All right, folks, you've got yourself a beautiful, flakey fish swimming in a bed of veggies and broth. Be careful when you open the pouch, the steam is very hot. Prepare to be delighted by the mouthwatering aroma of ginger, butter and seafood. Let's give it a squeeze of your second lemon wedge as a finishing touch. Serve it up with a side of crusty bread, which is great to have with it to soak up the flavorful broth, or with my staple starch—white rice.

~ LADY AND THE SCAMP ~

SHRIMP SCAMPI! Many people love to order this dish of garlic butter with shrimp and pasta from their favorite seafood restaurant, and I wanted to create the same restaurant-quality scampi at home. If you're not used to working with seafood, don't be intimidated, it's really quite simple to cook. I just made this last night and my tummy thanked me for it.

Serves 4

1¼ lb (560 g) shrimp, preferably jumbo 21–25 count or large 31–35 count, tails and shells on (see Flip Tip)

1 cup (240 ml) low sodium chicken or veggie broth

6 cloves garlic, minced, divided

4 tbsp (60 ml) olive oil, divided

¼ tsp salt

⅛ tsp freshly ground black pepper

1 medium heirloom or vine tomato, chopped

1 shallot, sliced

1 (5-oz [140-g]) bag fresh spinach

1 lb (454 g) dry linguini

Pinch of red pepper flakes

⅓ cup (80 ml) of your fave white wine (chardonnay is a safe bet)

1 cup (240 ml) freshly squeezed lemon juice (approximately 3 lemons)

1 tsp lemon zest

4 tbsp (56 g) salted butter

2 tbsp (8 g) fresh parsley, chopped, to serve

4 lemon wedges, to serve

FLIP TIP: Always ask your fish monger at the seafood section of your grocery about the size of a package of large or jumbo shrimp. There should be a 31–35 large or 21–25 jumbo individual shrimp per pound. I use 1¼ pounds (560 g) of jumbo shrimp in this recipe, enough for 4 people, so nobody will go home hungry!

Start by shelling the shrimp. Most of the time, shrimp has already been deveined or cleaned. If yours are not, just run a small knife on the outer curved part, and it should be a snap to clean out. You've got this.

For this recipe, I shell the body of the shrimp and leave the tail on. The shells of the shrimp have tons of flavor. I extract this flavor by simmering the shells in broth. Put the shells in a small sauce pan, then simmer them in the broth for about 2 to 3 minutes. Strain and discard the shells.

Time to marinate the shrimp. In a large bowl, combine the shrimp, 3 cloves of garlic, 1 tablespoon (15 ml) of the olive oil, and the salt and pepper. Mix and let marinate for 10 minutes.

While the shrimp is marinating, let's move on to a quick veggie sauté. In a large sauté pan, heat 2 tablespoons (30 ml) of olive oil over medium heat. Toss in the tomato and shallot, and cook for 3 to 4 minutes, until the shallot is translucent and tender and the tomato looks very soft. Now add in the entire bag of spinach. Yup, the whole bag. Sauté until the spinach wilts, which you will see happens very quickly. Scoop out the veggies, and set them aside.

The shrimp is really the star of the show, but if you need a good co-star, linguini is a hearty pasta that pairs nicely with its wide, flat shape. Just boil in salted water for 7 to 9 minutes for a perfecto al dente pasta.

Alrighty, the next contestant is the jumboooo shrimp. In the same pan you sautéed the veggies, turn up the heat again to medium, and toss in the marinated shrimp with all its juices for a quick cook. You are just trying to get a little flamingo-pink color on the shrimp, which only takes a couple minutes on each side. At this point, you're not going to cook them all the way through. Take out the shrimp and set them aside.

Leave all the juices and goodness in the pan and pour in the remaining 1 tablespoon (15 ml) of olive oil. The heat should be set to medium. Toss in the remaining garlic and my signature red pepper flakes, and stir for a minute to get those flavors warmed up in the oil. Add the wine, lemon juice, zest, and butter. Let all these amazing flavors party together 'til the butter is melted.

Now invite the shrimp back in, and pour in the shrimp-flavored broth. Reduce heat and continue cooking for 3 minutes. Add the sautéed veggies and mix. Turn off the heat, then toss in the pasta. Garnish with parsley and serve with 4 lemon wedges. See, wasn't that E-Z?!

Rice, of Course!

In my culture, a meal STARTS with rice. No matter what was cooking, there was always a pot of rice on perpetual standby in my house. I grew up eating rice with almost all of our meals. You'll find that one of my recipes is a quasi-rice dish, but I included it because rice is a necessary staple of the meal.

I have many a fond memory of growing up eating scoops and scoops of rice. Sometimes I'd mix it in with my eggs at breakfast, or I'd scoop a few spoonfuls into soup. There's really just no wrong time to add a bit of white rice to a meal.

So don't limit your rice consumption to the recipes in this section—as you "Flip" through this book, keep an eye out for more opportunities to swoop a scoop in!

~ ONE-POT CHOP SUEY ~

Anyone out there grow up eating frozen pot pies? My chicken chop suey is basically an Asian version of the classic pot pie—the pastry crust is just replaced with fluffy white rice. It's a hearty meal that's E-Z to assemble, and the extra oomph of Asian ingredients is so very satisfying to the taste buds.

Serves 4

MARINADE

3 tbsp (45 ml) rice wine vinegar

3 tbsp (45 ml) oyster sauce

1 tbsp (14 g) brown sugar

½ tsp salt

½ tsp freshly ground black pepper

3 tbsp (24 g) cornstarch

2 cups (280 g) sliced chicken (I like dark meat so I use 4 large chicken thighs, but for folks who prefer white meat, cut up 2 large chicken breasts)

CHOP SUEY

3 tbsp (45 ml) veggie oil, divided

Pinch of red pepper flakes

1 large Spanish onion, sliced

4 cloves garlic, minced

3 celery ribs, sliced on the bias (diagonally)

2 large carrots, julienned (cut into matchsticks)

⅓ Napa cabbage, sliced

1 (8-oz [227-g]) can water chestnuts, drained, sliced, optional

1 (8-oz [227-g]) can of bamboo shoots, drained, optional

1 (8-oz [227-g]) can baby corn, drained, optional

2 cups (140 g) fresh shiitake or cremini mushrooms, sliced and stems removed

1 cup (110 g) snap peas or sugar peas

1 cup (110 g) fresh soybean sprouts

1 tbsp (15 ml) sesame oil

2½ cups (600 ml) chicken broth (you can add ½ cup [120 ml] more broth if you love lots of sauce, like I do)

2 tbsp (30 ml) soy sauce

2 cups (400 g) white rice (Rice 101, page 56)

TOPPERS

3 green onions, trimmed, diced

Chicharrón, plain or spicy, cut into large pieces like croutons, optional

Fried chow mein noodles, optional

To make the marinade, combine the vinegar, oyster sauce, brown sugar, salt, pepper, and cornstarch in a bowl. Add the uncooked chicken. Cover and set in the fridge for 15 minutes.

Once the chicken is marinated, start the chop suey. Heat 2 tablespoons (30 ml) of the veggie oil in a wok or large sauté pan over medium-high heat. Add in the marinated chicken and cook for 5 minutes, mixing occasionally. Scoop out the chicken and set it aside.

Keeping the pan over medium-high heat, add the remaining veggie oil, red pepper flakes, and the entire veggie family of onion, garlic, celery, carrots, and cabbage, as well as the water chestnuts, bamboo shoots, and baby corn if you're using them. Sauté for 5 minutes. The goal is to retain the crispness of the vegetables, so we really need to cook them quickly—a process known as "flash-frying." Toss in the mushrooms, peas, soybean sprouts, and sesame oil. Although we're not using much sesame oil, this ingredient is so potent that a little bit goes a long way. Actually, it's used in Asian cooking as a seasoning rather than a cooking oil. I love it 'cause it really gives your dish that Asian twist. Honestly, to me, it wouldn't be chop suey without it.

Add the cooked chicken back in, along with the chicken broth and soy sauce. Mix well and simmer for another 5 minutes.

Can you believe it, your chop suey is good to go! Top it off with green onions, and even go crunchy with Chicharrón or fried chow mein noodles. What do you think we should serve it with? Drum roll, please . . . perhaps RICE?

~ RISOTTLO 'N' SEARED SCALLOPS ~

Creamy, savory rice with Parmesan and a hint of wine, paired with tender seared sea scallops—sounds like a romantic dinner for two at a fancy restaurant, right? Well now you make it in your own kitchen, and you can serve it to a crowd!

I know most people tend to steer clear of making risotto or scallops for themselves, let alone for a group of guests, but they're both actually quite E-Z to cook. The key to a good risotto is to start with a tasty veggie base, and then to build it up with a go-to wine and hearty broth.

Serves 4

2 tbsp (30 ml) olive oil

1 medium Vidalia onion, finely chopped (or 3 chopped shallots if you want a less potent onion)

4 cloves garlic, minced

½ tsp fresh thyme

12 baby bella mushrooms, sliced

1½ cups (300 g) arborio rice

6 tbsp (84 g) unsalted butter, divided

½ cup (120 ml) white wine

6 cups (1.4 L) chicken broth, divided

1½ cups (150 g) Parmigiano-Reggiano cheese, freshly grated, divided

1 lb (454 g) sea scallops, dried

Pinch of salt

Pinch of pepper

2 tbsp (30 ml) veggie oil

Lemon wedges, to serve

2 tbsp (8 g) fresh parsley, chopped

Start with a good pot. I use a Dutch oven, but any deep pot will do just fine. Heat the olive oil over medium heat, then add in the onion, garlic, and thyme. These aromatics are a terrific base combo for the rice. Sauté to get the onion translucent and tender, then add in the mushrooms and arborio rice. DON'T rinse the rice first, you want the starch for thickening when making risotto. Cook the rice and veggies for 2 minutes. In foodie talk, this step is called "toasting" the rice.

Add 2 tablespoons (28 g) of the butter, and pour in the white wine. Mix to coat the rice. The alcohol will cook off in about 1 minute, and will continue to evaporate while simmering in the hot liquid. At this point, we're just building up more flavor.

Time for the rice to go for a swim. Note that this is an unconventional way of cooking risotto; usually broth is added to the rice a little at a time, but my method is to cook the rice low-and-slow in a vat of broth. Warning: There are many stirring stages coming up to help keep the rice from sticking.

Let's begin by pouring 5 cups (1.2 L) of the broth into the pot of rice, and bringing it to a boil. Reduce the heat back to a simmer, and mix for a couple of minutes. Cover, allow it to cook for 7 minutes, then uncover and give it a quick stir. Cover again, and after another 7 minutes, stir. One more time now: Cover, and cook for 4 more minutes.

Turn off the heat and uncover the pot. Drop in another 2 tablespoons (28 g) of butter and fold in 1 cup (100 g) of the freshly grated Parmigiano-Reggiano cheese. Cover and let sit.

(continued)

Dry the scallops on both sides with paper towels. Season one side with the salt and pepper. Grab a large heavy-duty skillet—I use a cast iron one 'cause it's a great conductor of heat, and it's best to sear on a ripping hot skillet. Spread the veggie oil in the pan over high heat. Place each scallop in the skillet with the seasoned side facing down, making sure they are spaced evenly. Let the scallops sizzle and sear for 2 minutes, then season the second side and flip them. Sizzle and sear the second side for 2 minutes also, then turn off the heat. Add the remaining 2 tablespoons (28 g) of butter, and let it melt around the scallops for a minute.

Since the scallops cook in 5 minutes, the risotto should still be hot and ready to plate. If it seems too thick, use the remaining 1 cup (240 ml) of chicken broth to thin it out.

To serve, scoop up a spoonful of risotto, and nestle 4 or 5 scallops on the bed of risotto. Don't throw away the pan butter! Use it to top off the dish, along with a good squeeze of a lemon wedge, some of the remaining ½ cup (50 g) of Parmigiano-Reggiano cheese, and the fresh parsley.

Pat yourself on the back—you should be proud!

~ *ARROZ CALDO* ~
(CHICKEN RICE PORRIDGE)

I'm really excited to tell you how to make this recipe. Basically, it's my Momma's heal-all "congee," a broth or porridge made from rice and chicken broth, with some fun add-ons. It's a very common Filipino recipe, but since I was born in America I've Americanized it a bit. I do believe it has healing powers, 'cause whenever I'm down, or blue, or not feeling quite myself, this is the miracle cure to have in my belly.

Fun Fact: The ginger is cut into two chunks as part of a fun family superstition. If your bowl has a piece of ginger in it, a stroke of luck will be on its way!

Serves 6

1½ lb (680 g) chicken thighs (I like dark meat, but white meat will turn out just as yummy)

½ tsp salt, plus more to taste

¼ tsp freshly ground black pepper, plus more to taste

3 tbsp (45 ml) veggie oil, divided

1 medium onion, sliced

3 green onions, chopped, divided, whites for broth, greens for topper

3 celery ribs, chopped on the bias

3 large carrots, split, chopped on the bias

6 cloves garlic, minced

1 nub of fresh ginger, 1 inch (2.5 cm) minced, 1 inch (2.5 cm) cut in half, divided

8 cups (1.9 L) water

1 tbsp (16 g) chicken bouillon paste (I prefer paste over a dry bouillon cube)

1–2 tsp (5–10 ml) fish sauce (*patis*), optional (if you're not into it, sub 1 tbsp [15 ml] fresh lemon juice mixed with 1 tsp lime juice)

1 cup (186 g) cooked rice, long grained for more gluten

½ cup (120 ml) canola oil

½ cup (63 g) all-purpose flour

2 tbsp (16 g) cornstarch

4 fresh eggs

1 tsp white vinegar, divided

6 lemon wedges, to serve

Let's do an E-Z prep of the chicken. Peel the skins off the chicken thighs and set them aside to be used later. Lightly salt and pepper the chicken on all sides. The gizmo gadget of choice is my handy dandy pressure cooker. Add in 2 tablespoons (30 ml) of the veggie oil, and set the heat to medium. Brown the chicken thighs for a couple of minutes on each side, then take them out of the pot, and set them aside for a sec.

Heat up the remaining 1 tablespoon (15 ml) of veggie oil. Toss in the onion, the white parts of the green onions, and the celery, carrots, garlic, and minced ginger. Sauté for 5 minutes, until the onions are slightly translucent and tender. Scoop out half of the veggie sauté and set it aside.

Add the water and plop in the chicken bouillon paste. As I noted, I like paste better than dry bouillon, but if a cube is your go-to, I'll just look away. Now, this is completely optional: If you'd like to use it or have access to fish sauce, go ahead and add it in. If you're not into it, you can substitute a combo of lemon and lime juices. You will be missing out on a unique traditional Filipino flavor, though, folks!

Add the chicken thighs back into the pot, sprinkle with salt and pepper, and seal the lid to close up shop. Cook over low-medium heat for 15 minutes. Then release the steam and carefully open the pressure cooker to check on what's been brewing. The chicken should be soft, falling off the bone. Scoop the chicken out, debone it, and cut it up into chunks. Cover and set aside.

The smells of ginger, onion, and chicken should be wafting from the delicious broth. There may be a film of bubbles floating at the top of the broth, along the surface and sides of the pot. It's just protein residue, so scrape it up, scoop it out, and discard. Add in your cooked rice, the sautéed vegetables that you set aside, and the ginger chunks. Simmer on low for 25 minutes, stirring occasionally.

(continued)

ARROZ CALDO (CHICKEN RICE PORRIDGE)
(Continued)

What's that? You're wondering about the chicken skins, you say? OK, let's start frying. Heat the canola oil in a skillet over medium-high heat. Mix the flour with the cornstarch, and dredge the skins. Fry them until they're crispy, and drain them on a paper towel. Now you've got crackling!

Ring-a-ding-ding, the 25 minutes are up. Add the deboned chicken chunks back into your pot. We're in the home stretch, you guys!

Typically eggs aren't served with this dish, but I discovered that a poached egg adds another level of creaminess, so I tweaked the traditional recipe. In a small saucepan filled about two-thirds of the way with water, add the vinegar and a pinch of salt, and heat to a gentle simmer. I like to first crack the egg in a separate bowl, in case of shell mishaps. Cooking 1 egg at a time, I use the old whirlpool-vortex technique. I swirl the simmering water with a spoon, then pour the egg into the center of the whirling water. The submerged egg will slowly cook over approximately 3 minutes. Scoop it out with a spoon, and voilà!—a beautifully poached egg. Repeat the process per serving.

To serve, ladle a hearty helping of the *Arroz Caldo* into a serving bowl. Add the poached egg, green onions, a squeeze from a wedge of lemon, and the crispy skin cracklings.

Enjoy, and look out for the lucky ginger!

~ FRIED RICE FRENZY ~

Fried rice, in all honesty, is an everything-but-the-kitchen-sink type of recipe. For a Filipino cook like me, this dish starts with a good base of rice seasoned with garlic and salt, and then every time I make it, I add something different—a meat, a seafood, or a few more veggies. Reinventing the dish constantly is fun for me because it allows me to be creative, and it's a great dish for beginners to play around with to suit your family's tastes. That's what I like about Fried Rice Frenzy—there's just no wrong way to cook it up.

Serves 4

4 slices bacon

½ Spanish onion, chopped

Pinch of red pepper flakes

2 cloves garlic, minced

3 cups (558 g) day-old cooked rice

½ tsp salt, plus more to taste

2 tbsp (28 g) butter, divided

2 cups (182 g) cooked assorted veggies

1 cup (150 g) cooked sirloin steak, cubed

1 cup (100 g) cooked shrimp, 8–10 pieces, cut in halves

2 eggs

½ tsp garlic powder, optional

¼ tsp freshly ground black pepper

There are a few essential ingredients that I like to start out with as a good base. *Numero uno* is day-old rice. Leftover rice is *muy importante*, because its lack of moisture allows it to fry up nicely. The last thing you want is soggy fried rice. The second ingredient is definitely an onion of some sort. Take your pick—Spanish, Vidalia, red, shallots, or even green onions. Garlic makes the list of necessities as number 3. Although I prefer fresh cloves of garlic, I certainly wouldn't turn my nose up at the convenience of dried garlic powder. I use it often. And last but certainly not least, you need salt. Yup, these four ingredients make a good base for a great-tasting fried rice.

So what next? What I do is open my fridge and scan the various types of leftovers I'd like to use up. I don't like to waste anything. Go ahead—look for some protein and some veggies. You can start with the ingredients I've listed.

To follow this recipe, heat up a large skillet or wok over medium-high heat, and fry up the bacon, which will render fat that will be used to sauté the onion. Set the bacon aside.

Let's get the onion cooking in the bacon fat. If I didn't have bacon, then 3 to 4 tablespoons (45 to 60 ml) of veggie oil would do. Add in good ol' red pepper flakes, and plop in the garlic. Sauté with the heat on medium, making sure the garlic doesn't burn.

All right, add in the day-old rice. With a spoon, or a handy dandy spatula, mix and push down on the rice in a smashing and smushing action. The goal is to separate all the clumped-together rice so that every grain picks up the onion, garlic, and bacon flavors. I add about ½ teaspoon of salt as I continue to mix and smush the rice.

(continued)

Finally, the star of the show is going into the wok! Incorporate the rice thoroughly with the rest of the ingredients. Sauté for 5 minutes, giving the rice a slight toast.

Time for some wine—but it's for deglazing, not drinking. Pour in the wine and scrape the bottom of the pan to loosen up all the flavorful bits. Now pour in 2½ cups (600 ml) of the shrimp and chicken broth mix. Bring it to a boil while stirring occasionally to prevent the rice from sticking. Add the juice of half a lemon and the parsley, then reduce the heat to medium-low. Mix well just ONCE more. This will be the last time the rice will be mixed. Cook for 15 minutes, allowing most of the liquid to absorb into the rice.

Nestle the shrimp, mussels, and clams in the rice throughout the pan. Add the remaining ½ cup (120 ml) of broth mix, set the heat to the lowest setting, and cook for another 10 minutes, uncovered.

The rice should not be mushy; it should have an al dente bite to it. Also, a crispy browned crust of caramelized rice should have formed on the bottom of the pan. This is a GOOD THING. It's called *socarrat*, and it's what you want in your paella. Listen for a crackling sound when all the liquid has cooked off. Turn off the heat and let it sit in the pan for 3 to 4 minutes.

I like to garnish with buttery peas, and don't forget the chorizo. Serve with lemon wedges and hot sauce. Scoop some up, it's party time!

FLIP TIP: The common French veggie base combo of onion, celery, and carrots is called a *mirepoix*. There's also the Cajun Holy Trinity where the seasoning veggies are onion, celery, and bell pepper. Here's one more for you, folks: Spain's combo is garlic, onion, and celery, called *sofrito*.

Gotta Use Your Noodle

Believe me, I've had my fair share of days feeling sick of the same old meals. I've caught myself just staring into the pantry, waiting for a spark of food inspiration. After boiling over countless ideas, I would see it—a lonely box of pasta in the back of my cupboard. Perhaps a pastafest? A party of plates filled with oodles of noodles, dressed in a red or white sauce, dancing over an array of sautéed vegetables?

I'm sure you all have that extra just-in-case pasta box sitting around, so let's jazz up these family recipes with fun and creative twists. When you're tired of the same kit and caboodle, don't go crazy, just use your noodle!

~ LO'S NO BAKE RICH 'N' CREAMY ~ MAC 'N' CHEEZY

It was a no brainer to put three of my favorite cheeses together in one dish. I mean, c'mon. These particular cheeses combine well and melt beautifully together: Buttery, aged cheddar is gooey and rich, Monterey Jack is mellow and smooth, and Gruyère is a tangy, complex cheese that blends smoothly with the other two.

There are a few things that make my mac 'n' cheese stand out. I infused the liquid ingredients with fresh garlic—I could just as easily have called the recipe Garlic Mac 'n' Cheez. And my evaporated milk and heavy cream combo makes it creamier than other recipes that call for just milk. Rather than the traditional elbow macaroni, I use the swirly tubed Cavatappi pasta to capture even more cheese sauce inside every noodle. It's the best "no bake" you'll ever make!

Serves 12

3 tbsp (24 g) plus ¼ tsp kosher salt, divided	2 cups (226 g) white medium sharp cheddar cheese (grate it yourself, peeps, it makes for a creamier sauce)
½ lb (227 g) Cavatappi pasta	
9 tbsp (126 g) unsalted butter, divided	2 cups (226 g) Gruyère cheese (again, grate it yourself for a creamier sauce; see Flip Tip)
7 large cloves garlic, minced	
¼ tsp onion powder	1 cup (113 g) Monterey Jack cheese (grate it yourself!)
¼ tsp salt	
¼ tsp freshly ground black pepper	½ cup (28 g) Panko Japanese breadcrumbs
¼ tsp smoked paprika, optional	¼ cup (27 g) seasoned Italian breadcrumbs
Pinch of nutmeg, optional	8 slices of cooked bacon, cut into ½-inch (1.3-cm) pieces, optional
Pinch of dried thyme, optional	
2 cups (480 ml) evaporated milk	4 plum tomatoes, seeded, chopped into small cubes, optional
1 cup (240 ml) heavy cream	3 green onions, chopped, optional

In a large pot, boil enough water to cover your pasta. Salt the water with 3 tablespoons (24 g) salt. The cheeses have salt in them, so I don't make the water as salty as I would when making other pasta. Cook for 10 minutes, stirring occasionally, to an al dente texture—meaning just long enough so that the pasta is neither hard nor soft, but has a bite to it. Confirm the texture by carefully taking a noodle out to taste test. Once the pasta is al dente, take the pot off the heat, strain the water out, then place the pasta back into the same pot.

In a separate pot over low heat, melt 6 tablespoons (84 g) of the butter and sauté your garlic, onion powder, ¼ teaspoon salt, pepper, the paprika, nutmeg, and thyme, if using, then stir. Pour in the evaporated milk and heavy cream, and mix well.

Here's the best part—start adding your cheese 1 cup (113 g) at a time. Don't rush it, keep it LO-and-slow. Just heat and mix for a few minutes until all of the cheese is melted and blended.

Now it's time for the pasta to SWIM in the creamy, cheese sauce. Slowly pour or scoop the strained pasta into the pot of cheese. Using a rubber spatula, fold in the pasta until it's totally combined.

Grease a 9 x 13-inch (23 x 33-cm) baking dish or a casserole dish at least 3 inches (8 cm) deep with either a nonstick cooking spray or a chunk of butter (I do the latter). Carefully transfer your pot of gold into the baking dish.

Mix together the Panko Japanese breadcrumbs and the seasoned Italian breadcrumbs. Sprinkle the mix on top of the mac 'n' cheese. Melt the remaining 3 tablespoons (45 ml) of the butter and drizzle it over the crumbs. Set the oven on high broil and place the dish under the broiler. It only takes a few minutes to brown the bubbly, crunchy top layer, but the exact timing depends on your oven strength, so keep an eye on it, folks. Look for the breadcrumb mix to turn a nice golden brown.

Indulge yourself with a scoop of this super creamy, comfort food with optional toppers of chopped bacon, tomatoes, and green onions. OMG, to me it's heaven in a bowl! BOOYAH people!

FLIP TIP: If you don't mind processed cheese, you can substitute the Gruyère for 1 (16-oz [453-g]) block of cubed Velveeta cheese to get that great melt.

～ *BOOLA BOOLA* STEW ～
(SHROOMS 'N' BEEF)

Why it's called *boola boola* is a mystery to me, but I remember always being so excited to eat this beef dinner with yummy mushrooms and noodles stewed in a rich, buttery brown gravy. I suppose it's a comfort food similar to turkey and gravy for some folks. I always felt like my Momma was treating us to something special when she served this.

Serves 4 to 6

2 tbsp (30 ml) veggie oil, divided

2 cups (285 g) sirloin steak, thinly sliced (freeze the meat for about 1 hour first for easier slicing)

3 tbsp (24 g) plus ½ tsp kosher salt, divided

¼ tsp freshly ground black pepper, divided

2 pinches of red pepper flakes

1 large Spanish onion, sliced

¾ stick (84 g) salted butter, room temp, divided

10 fresh shiitake mushrooms, sliced

1 (10-oz [283-g]) package cremini mushrooms, sliced in halves (see Flip Tip)

2 cups (480 ml) beef broth

1 (12-oz [340-g]) package of wide egg noodles

2 tbsp (16 g) cornstarch

2 tbsp (30 ml) water

Hot sauce, optional

In a large skillet or wok, heat 1 tablespoon (15 ml) of veggie oil over high heat. I like to sear the meat quickly on high. This will be done in two batches: Sear 1 cup (142 g) of the beef at a time, adding ¼ teaspoon of salt and ⅛ teaspoon of pepper per batch. Cook for 2 to 3 minutes, then place the seared beef in a bowl.

It's time to sauté the lovely vegetables. First, you must reduce the heat to medium, then add the other tablespoon (15 ml) of veggie oil. Toss in my signature red pepper flakes, then drop in the onion and sauté for 2 to 3 minutes to sweat out the natural sugars. Make sure not to brown the onion—you just want it to be translucent and tender.

Now add ½ stick (56 g) of butter. Once it's melted, add in the duo of mushrooms. Sauté for another 5 minutes.

Home stretch folks! Let's add the beef back in, then pour in the beef broth. Bring to a boil, cover, and simmer over low heat for 1½ hours. Sounds long, but trust me, it'll be worth it.

In the last 20 minutes of simmering, you should grab another medium pot to start boiling water for your egg noodles. Fill up a large pot two-thirds full of water and add 3 tablespoons (24 g) kosher salt. Once the water boils, add your egg noodles and stir immediately to help prevent clumping. Cook for about 5 minutes, then drain. Pour the noodles back into the pot, add the remaining butter, and stir.

There should be about 5 minutes left on your simmering timer. This is when you should make your slurry, then add it to the broth to thicken it. Mix the cornstarch and water and add it to the beef broth.

Turn off the heat and scoop the buttered noodles into the simmering pot of beef and veggies. HELLOOOO Boola!

Take in the aroma of that beautifully rich combination of buttery beef and smokey mushrooms. Scoop some stew into a bowl and add a dash of hot sauce, if using. Told you it was worth the wait!

FLIP TIP: Cremini mushrooms are firmer and have a better flavor than younger white shrooms. They're used frequently in stews and soups because they hold up better in liquid.

PEPPERONI LASAGNA

This recipe is for the home cooks who want to make lasagna with an old-fashioned, homemade sauce. If you have a favorite jarred sauce, feel free to swap that in, but I like my recipes to have as many homemade ingredients as possible.

So, why pepperoni? The answer is simple—when it cooks, it renders delicious oils that add tons of flavor. I love it!

Serves 8

HOMEMADE SAUCE

1 (28-oz [794-g]) can peeled, whole San Marzano tomatoes (see Flip Tip)

1 (12-oz [340-g]) can tomato paste

2 cups (480 ml) water

2 tbsp (30 ml) veggie oil

1 large Vidalia onion, minced

1 small carrot, diced

Pinch of red pepper flakes

½ lb (227 g) ground beef, 80% lean 20% fat

½ lb (227 g) ground hot Italian sausage

1 tsp salt

¼ tsp freshly ground black pepper

6 cloves garlic, minced

1 tsp dried oregano

1 tsp dried basil

1 cup (138 g) pepperoni, chopped

RICOTTA MIX

1 lb (454 g) ricotta cheese

½ cup (50 g) Romano cheese (Parmesan is a good substitute)

1 lb (454 g) grated mozzarella cheese, divided, plus more for garnish (see Flip Tip)

1 tbsp (4 g) fresh parsley, chopped

PASTA

¼ cup (32 g) kosher salt

1 box dry lasagna noodles

2 tbsp (3 g) fresh basil, roughly chopped

For the homemade sauce, start by pureeing the tomatoes, tomato paste, and water in a large mixing bowl. In other words, mash them to the consistency of a liquid or creamy paste. I have a handy dandy hand-held immersion blender to use in the bowl, but if you don't have one you can use a regular drink blender too.

In a large stock pot, add the oil and sauté the onion, carrot, and red pepper flakes. When the veggies appear translucent and tender, add the ground beef and sausage. Do your best to break up the sausage, since it tends to stick together. Season with the salt and pepper. Cook until the meat is browned, then add the garlic into the mix. I add the garlic last to avoid burning it, which I have done a million times.

Pour the puree mix into the pot and simmer for 1½ hours. You can realistically cook the sauce a shorter period of time, maybe a minimum of 45 minutes, but the longer you cook it the better it tastes—so I say stew away. Taste test the mix at 30 minutes, 1 hour, and 1½ hours. Yum, yummy, yummier, right?

Now for the ricotta prep. Combine the ricotta, Romano, ¼ pound (112 g) of the mozzarella, and parsley in a bowl.

Fast forward . . . The sauce is ready. Let's preheat the oven to 350°F (177°C) and move on to the pasta. Fill a pot two-thirds full of water, and add the kosher salt and bring to a boil. Drop in the full box of dry lasagna pasta sheets. You may not end up using them all, I just like to have a few extra in case any break. Boil for 10 minutes, stirring occasionally to prevent the pasta from sticking together. Drain, and lay the pasta sheets out on a clean kitchen towel to absorb excess moisture.

All right, this is the fun part, so roll up your sleeves, wash your hands, and prepare to assemble. First you need to add a few things to the stewed sauce. Mix in the dried oregano and dried basil, and you CAN'T forget the pepperoni. I add these guys in at the end to avoid bitterness developing from long stewing of the spices, and to prevent overcooking the pepperoni.

In a 13 x 9 x 3–inch (33 x 23 x 8–cm) baking dish, scoop in ⅓ of the sauce for the bottom layer of the lasagna. Next, place a layer of pasta noodles side by side—three strips should fit perfectly, and don't worry if you overlap. Add a thin layer of the ricotta mix. Repeat the layering, starting with the sauce again. Just make sure you end with a final layer of sauce that will be topped off with the reserved mozzarella cheese.

Cover the lasagna with aluminum foil and bake on the middle rack of the oven for 15 minutes. Then remove the foil and finish baking for 45 minutes. Let it rest for 11 minutes (my lucky number!). Top with the fresh basil, and enjoy your masterpiece!

FLIP TIPS: When looking for canned tomatoes, look for San Marzanos. They are the best plum tomatoes known from Italy. It's a sweeter tomato with minimal seeds and is low in acidity.

I use a harder block of mozzarella so it's easier to grate. If you like using a fresh ball of mozzarella, just cut it in half, grate half, and slice the other for the lasagna topper.

~ PANCIT CANTON ~
(FILIPINO NOODLES)

Pancit is a popular Filipino noodle dish, and the type of noodle is what differentiates *Pancit Canton* from *Pancit Bihon*. *Bihon* are rice noodles, and *canton* are flour noodles. You can use a mix of both, the combo is delicious, but for this recipe I'm just using canton. It's a soft, buttery, stir-fry flour noodle, and is often described as a cousin to lo mein. This noodle is like Rogue from *X-Men*—it absorbs flavors and takes on the characteristics of whatever ingredients it touches! But don't worry if you can't make it to your local Asian market, I'll also show you how to swap it out for spaghetti noodles.

Serves 8

I'm a true believer in a good marination, but in traditional Filipino *pancit* there is no marination step. My tweak to this recipe IS to marinate. Toss the chicken into a large bowl. Add the soy sauce and oyster sauce, followed by the nontraditional ingredients of brown sugar, ginger powder, and vinegar. Mix well, making sure the meat is submerged in the marinade, then cover and set aside for 30 minutes.

Now for the shrimp prep. Traditional *pancit* recipes cook with oil, garlic, salt, and pepper. My twist is to use these ingredients for the shrimp marinade. Combine the veggie oil with the garlic, lemon juice, salt, and pepper. Throw in the shrimp, allow it to swim in the marinade, cover and set aside.

If you have no canton noodles, this is the time to make the spaghetti. Cook the pasta in boiling water for 6 to 7 minutes, until it is seriously al dente, then set it aside.

For the canton noodles, pour the chicken broth into a deep pot and heat to a boil. Turn the heat down to simmer and drop in the dry canton noodles. Allow them to soak up most of the broth, about 10 minutes. If you're using spaghetti noodles, heat up only 1 cup (240 ml) of broth and add the cooked noodles. Simmer until they have absorbed most of the broth.

At this point the chicken should have been marinating for about 30 minutes, so we're ready to cook it up. If you have a wok, use it. If not, you'll need a large pot or a deep pan. Heat the wok over medium heat. Using a slotted spoon, scoop the chicken from its marinade and place it into the hot wok. Cook the chicken for 5 to 7 minutes, mixing occasionally.

(continued)

CHICKEN MARINADE

4–5 skinless chicken thighs, deboned and chopped into chunks

¼ cup (60 ml) soy sauce

2 tbsp (30 ml) oyster sauce

2 tbsp (28 g) brown sugar

¼ tsp ginger powder

1 tbsp (15 ml) white vinegar or rice wine vinegar

SHRIMP MARINADE

¼ cup (60 ml) veggie oil

4 cloves garlic, minced

Juice of ½ a lemon

¼ tsp salt

¼ tsp pepper

½ lb (227 g) jumbo shrimp, 21–25 count, shelled and deveined

NOODLES

4 cups (960 ml) low sodium chicken broth

1 (8-oz [227-g]) package of dry canton flour noodles or ⅔ box of spaghetti noodles

1 medium onion, sliced

2 carrots, thinly chopped

1 cup (110 g) green beans, cut on the bias into 1-inch (2.5-cm) slices

8 fresh shiitake mushrooms, sliced

⅓ head of a small green cabbage, shredded or chopped

2 green onions, green portion cut to 1 inch (2.5 cm)

Juice of ½ a lemon

2 tsp (10 ml) fish sauce, *patis*

TOPPERS

12 snap peas, quickly sautéed with salt and pepper

4 hard-boiled eggs, sliced

4 Chinese sausages, fried, sliced on the bias

½ a lemon, wedged

Chicharrón, chopped

PANCIT CANTON (FILIPINO NOODLES)
(Continued)

Moving on to cooking the veggies! First spoon 2 tablespoons (30 ml) of the shrimp marinade into the wok. Leaving the heat on medium, add the onion, carrots, green beans, shiitake mushrooms, cabbage, and green onions. Sauté the veggies for 5 to 7 minutes.

Now the shrimp, including its remaining marinade, joins the party in the wok. Pour in the lemon juice and *patis*. The fish sauce may be substituted with 1 tablespoon (15 ml) of oyster sauce.

Transfer the noodles into the wok. Combine them well, tossing everything together.

I like presenting this dish in a large oval platter. If you want to go full Flip, use all of the toppers to decorate—snap peas, hard-boiled eggs, Chinese sausage, lemon wedges, and Chicharrón.

You did it! You just made one of the most popular Filipino noodle dishes!

MEATBALL SPAGHETTS

People ask me this one spaghetti question all the time: Do I prefer cooking up a bolognese sauce or meatballs and sauce? Well, I say meatballs and sauce all the way. Why? Basically 'cause I can use meatballs for more than just one dinner—I can use leftovers for a meatball eggplant parm, a meatball casserole, or a huge meatball sandwich. Oh man, just thinking about a meatball sandwich, with some provolone cheese and extra sauce, is driving me bonkers. Come to think of it, I may have cooked up a meatball pizza or even a meatball egg roll at least once in my lifetime.

Serves 6 to 8

MEATBALLS

4 tbsp (60 ml) olive oil, divided

Pinch of red pepper flakes

1 Spanish onion, finely chopped

3 cloves garlic, finely minced

1 lb (454 g) ground beef, 80% lean 20% fat

1 lb (454 g) ground sweet or hot sausage

7 fresh basil leaves, torn or chopped

¼ tsp dried basil

1 cup (56 g) Panko Japanese breadcrumbs

1 cup (100 g) Parmigiano-Reggiano cheese, grated

2 eggs

½ tsp salt

¼ tsp freshly ground black pepper

SAUCE

2 (28-oz [794-g]) cans peeled whole San Marzano tomatoes

2 tbsp (30 ml) extra virgin olive oil, if needed

Pinch of red pepper flakes, optional

1 medium Spanish onion, chopped

½ medium carrot, grated

4 cloves garlic, minced

1½ tsp (3 g) dried oregano

½ tsp salt

¼ tsp freshly ground black pepper

Parmesan rind, optional

¼ cup (60 ml) pasta water

SPAGHETTI

¼ cup (32 g) kosher salt

1–2 boxes dry spaghetti noodles (1 box of spaghetti serves 4–6, but the sauce yield in this recipe serves 6–8)

Let's start putting together these awesome meatballs. Grab your go-to large sauté pan or deep pot and heat up 1 tablespoon (30 ml) of olive oil over medium heat. Add the red pepper flakes, onion, and garlic and sauté for just 5 minutes, then set aside to cool. I just like to cook them enough to mellow out the flavors of the fresh veggies, and in doing this, add a different layer of flavor to the meatballs.

Grab a large mixing bowl and roll up your sleeves, it's time to get down and dirty mixing up some meatballs. Have a bowl of cold water nearby to wet your hands with before rolling each meatball. Using your hands, mix and combine the ground beef, sausage, fresh and dried basil, breadcrumbs, cheese, eggs, salt and pepper, as well as the cooled onion and garlic. It's OK to refrigerate the mix before forming your meatballs, but I like to get to it straight away. Form balls slightly bigger than a golf ball; you can use a ¼-cup (60-ml) ice cream scoop to help. I can get about 1 dozen meatballs made with this recipe.

Now that the meatballs are formed, the next step is to brown them up. Heat up a deep pot over medium-high heat. Add in the remaining 3 tablespoons (30 ml) of olive oil, and wait until a shimmering sheen ripples through the oil before adding the formed meatballs into the pot. Don't burn your meatballs, folks. Brown the meatballs evenly by turning them once or twice. Don't go anywhere, the cook time is only 10 minutes. When finished, place them on a plate with a loose tent of aluminum foil. This will not only keep them warm, but it will allow the meatballs to continue to cook until they're transferred into the sauce.

Moving on to the sauce, prep the tomatoes by pouring them into a big bowl and smashing them with a fork. My method is to just crush them by hand. Make sure to save all the juices from the can.

(continued)

MEATBALL SPAGHETTS (Continued)

Heat the meatball pot again over medium heat. There should be a good amount of rendered oil left from browning the meatballs. If not, add the olive oil, the red pepper flakes, if using, and the onion and carrot. Sauté for 5 minutes until the veggies are translucent and tender, then add the garlic.

Carefully pour in the bowl of crushed tomatoes with all the juice. Add in the oregano, salt, pepper, and Parmesan rind if you're using it. Turn down the heat to low and simmer for 15 minutes, LO-and-slow here, folks. If the sauce is simmered too long or if the heat is too high it will thicken up. No worries, you'll be able to thin it out later using the pasta water reserved in the next step.

While the sauce is simmering away, it's a good time to get some water boiling for the pasta. Fill a deep pot two-thirds full of water. Add the kosher salt and bring the water to a boil. Once the water is boiling at a rumble, add the pasta and immediately stir so the spaghetti noodles don't stick together. Cook for 7 to 9 minutes, or follow the box instructions for al dente cooking. Reserve ¼ cup (60 ml) of pasta water for the sauce, then drain the rest.

Check on the sauce to see how thick it is. Typically it does thicken up a little too much for me, so before I add the browned meatballs, I add the reserved pasta water. Then it's time to add those awesome meatballs you made! Simmer the whole mix for 10 more minutes, and then YOU ARE DONE!

Serve this dish with a fresh garden salad and some crunchy Italian bread, or better yet, an over-the-top buttery, CHEEZY garlic bread. Yowza, that sounds good!

MOMMA'S *MAMI* SOUP
(FILIPINO CHICKEN SOUP)

Mami is a soup that I grew up on—it's my Momma's Filipino chicken soup recipe. When she made this soup, I was always in charge of the toppers, which at the time I thought was just no fun. Little did I know that one of the toppers was actually the most important ingredient . . . TOASTED GARLIC. Yup, that's the secret. It adds a distinct nutty, buttery garlic flavor to the homemade chicken stock. I tell ya, without the garlic, my dad won't eat it. So getting the garlic toasted successfully was the deciding factor on whether my family was going to have Mami for dinner or not. Should you choose to accept this responsibility, the fate of your taste buds is entirely in your hands.

Serves 6 to 8

1 head of garlic, peeled and minced

5 cups (1.2 L) low sodium chicken broth, divided

2 tbsp (30 ml) veggie oil

Pinch of red pepper flakes

1 medium Spanish onion, sliced

3 carrots, diced or roughly chopped, peeling optional

3 celery ribs, sliced thinly on the bias

3 tbsp (24 g) plus ½ tsp kosher salt, divided

¼ tsp freshly ground black pepper

1 chicken breast or 5 chicken thighs

4 cups (960 ml) water

3 tbsp (45 ml) soy sauce, divided

4 eggs

¾ lb (340 g) dry elbow macaroni or 1 bag of egg noodles

5 green onions, chopped

Let's do it. Here is my sure-fire technique to a perfect toasted garlic. Mince the cloves of garlic to smithereens, but don't smash or macerate them.

Spray a medium-sized nonstick skillet with cooking spray. The heat will be set to low for the entire 14-minute toasting. DO NOT RUSH THE COOKING PROCESS. Spread the garlic in an even layer throughout the pan. Set a timer for 7 minutes, and leave it be. After 7 minutes, stir the garlic around and again spread it out evenly. Set the timer for 4 minutes. Let the garlic continue to toast UNTOUCHED. A lovely aroma of garlic should be filling the air. After the 4 minutes, stir and spread the garlic again, and set the timer for 3 minutes. During this period, the garlic aroma will change to a toasted, nutty aroma. Turn off the heat and pull the pan away from the stove. Shimmy and shake the pan in the air like you're making Jiffy Pop. Oh, did I just date myself? Well, just shake the pan around to allow the garlic to move about the pan. Transfer the toasted garlic onto a paper towel-lined plate, letting it air dry and cool. Mission accomplished!

Before moving on to the rest of the recipe, let's deglaze the pan used to make the toasted garlic by pouring in 2 cups (480 ml) of chicken broth. It would be silly to waste the flavor bits left in the pan. Set it aside for use later.

Alrighty then, now find yourself a humongous pot for the veggies. I like to just sweat them. Heat up the veggie oil and red pepper flakes over medium heat. Add the onion, carrots, celery, ½ teaspoon salt, and pepper. Let them cook for a few minutes, then scoop them out and set them aside.

(continued)

RAMEN NOMADINGDONG (Continued)

Fast forward 1 day . . . Drain the marinade from the beef. Heat the veggie oil in a large skillet over medium-high heat, and cook the meat for 3 minutes on each side. Set aside.

Next up is the broth. Grab your favorite soup pot and heat the oil over medium heat. Add the red pepper flakes, onion, shiitake mushrooms, ginger, garlic, and tomatoes, and sauté for 5 to 7 minutes. Once the tomatoes have softened, or melted down as I call it, add in the *patis*, if using, both the beef and chicken broths, and the baby bok choy segments if you're using them. Keep the veggies on a low simmer while you cook the noodles, about 11 minutes. Don't worry, I didn't forget the shrimp—I like to add that in at the end.

Now let's get going on our noodle hack. Fill a pot with the water and bring it to boil. No need to salt the water. Add in the baking soda and then the spaghetti noodles. Cook for 11 minutes, then strain and rinse the noodles with water.

Turn the heat on the pot of broth back up to medium. I like to wait 'til the broth starts to ripple, then the shrimp goes in for a light swim. Simmer for 4 minutes, and once the shrimp turns a pretty orange, it's ready to get in your belly. I prefer the shell-on shrimp 'cause it adds more flavor to the broth. It may be a bit of trouble to shell shrimp when eating a soup, but I think of it as unwrapping a treat.

Alrighty, it's assembly time. Fill up your bowl in this order: meat, noodles, broth, sprouts, eggs, a few dashes of sesame oil, green onions, and sprinkle on some toasted sesame seeds. Bib up and SLURP away!

~ ALL-4-ME CREAM-FREE ~ FETTUCCINE

I have to say, when a plate of fettuccine is placed in front of me, you might as well not talk to me 'til after the meal. Back in my 20s I ate mounds of the creamy noodles once a week. Unfortunately, the heavy cream was too much for my tummy to handle, so I had to find an alternative way of feeding my face with fettuccine. Luckily for me, I'm pretty crafty in the kitchen and was able to whip up this tummy-friendly version.

Serves 4

¼ cup (32 g) kosher salt

1 lb (454 g) fettuccine noodles (try 8 oz [227 g] of white and 8 oz [227 g] of green fettuccine)

1 cup (240 ml) low sodium chicken or veggie broth

1 stick (114 g) unsalted butter, cut into 8 butter tabs

1 cup (100 g) freshly grated Parmigiano-Reggiano or Parmesan cheese, divided

Fresh black pepper, to taste

2 tbsp (2 g) fresh parsley, chopped

Fill a large pot two-thirds full of water, add the kosher salt, and bring to a boil. Once it's boiling, submerge the fettuccine, stirring right away to prevent the pasta from sticking together. Cook for 8 to 10 minutes, until the pasta is al dente. Drain, reserving 2 cups (480 ml) of the pasta water.

The pasta will still need additional salt after it's cooked. I try to be creative by adding more flavor and saltiness with the addition of chicken broth instead of straight up salt. Pour 1 cup (240 ml) of the reserved pasta water with the chicken broth into a large sauté pan. Simmer over low heat, whisking continuously, and add in the butter tabs one at a time to gradually melt them. Oh geez, what did you do? Does the liquid look like a watery, cloudy mess? No worries, it's supposed to look this way. Sift about ¾ cup (75 g) cup of cheese into the pool of cloudy, buttery liquid a little bit at a time, maintaining your constant whisking.

Let's invite the pasta to the party. Add all the pasta to the creamy cheese sauce, and mix well. Eyeball the pasta—if the sauce looks watery, add some of the remaining Parmesan; if the sauce seems loose or thick, add a few tablespoons (15 to 45 ml) of the remaining cup (240 ml) of pasta water.

Plate the dish by using tongs to nestle the fettuccine into your favorite pasta bowl. Spoon in some sauce, crack in a bit of freshly ground pepper, and sprinkle on some fresh parsley. Top it off with the extra cheese, and that's it!

Hello, Sweet Tooth!

Willy Wonka & the Chocolate Factory happens to be one of my top ten FAVORITE movies of all time. It brings back some of the best memories of my childhood, and changed the course of my sweet tooth F O R E V E R.

How so, you ask? Well, just in case you didn't know, the movie is about a magical factory, and hidden within it, a fantastical world made almost ENTIRELY out of candy. After watching the kids in the movie sample Wonka's wondrous delights, I wanted to taste every sweet imaginable.

This chapter highlights my affinity for sweets. Although I may not be able to make a world completely out of chocolate, I created a chapter filled with scrumptious treats. I've got your golden ticket!

LECHE FLANTASTIC
(CARAMEL CUSTARD)

When I was little, I couldn't get enough of this homemade Filipino dessert, *leche flan*. It's a delicious custard pudding topped with a blanket of caramel. I suppose you could say it's a cousin of crème brûlée, which is also made of custard, but what makes flan different is its hard caramel topper. I can thank my Tita Tessie for the first flan I ever tasted. Her take on this dessert was a great base to work from in developing my own recipe. This one's for you, Tita Tessie!

Yields 8 to 12 slices

CARAMEL

⅔ cup (132 g) white granulated sugar

2 tbsp (30 ml) water

CUSTARD

8 egg yolks (see Flip Tip)

1 (14-oz [414-ml]) can condensed milk

1 (14-oz [414-ml]) can evaporated milk

2 tsp (10 ml) vanilla extract

1 tsp fresh lemon juice

First things first, preheat the oven to 350°F (177°C).

For the caramel, set a pan on a burner on THE LOWEST heat setting. Pour the sugar in and spread it evenly in the pan, then add the water. In about 3 minutes, the sugar and water mix should start to bubble. By minute 6, crystal snow should form as the water begins to evaporate. Look for an amber color to develop as the mix starts to liquify, around minute 7 or 8.

Lift the sauce pan off the heat, but hold it above the burner. Swirl the mix in a circular motion for 30 seconds—DON'T mix with a utensil. Place the pan back on the heat for another 30 seconds, then turn it off. Repeat the lift and swirl technique until all the crystals are melted—it will take a minute. The entire process should take a total of about 10 minutes, and don't second guess the timing, the sugar crystals WILL melt. You should end up with a deep amber-colored caramel syrup.

Immediately pour the syrup into a 9-inch (23-cm) round Pyrex glass baking dish, and begin to tilt and swirl the dish around to get the caramel to coat the bottom and the sides. Don't worry if the coating only reaches one-third to halfway up the sides. Timing is important here—this has to be a quick step, 'cause the syrup solidifies FAST! And please be very careful, as the only thing worse than burning the caramel is burning yourself!

(continued)

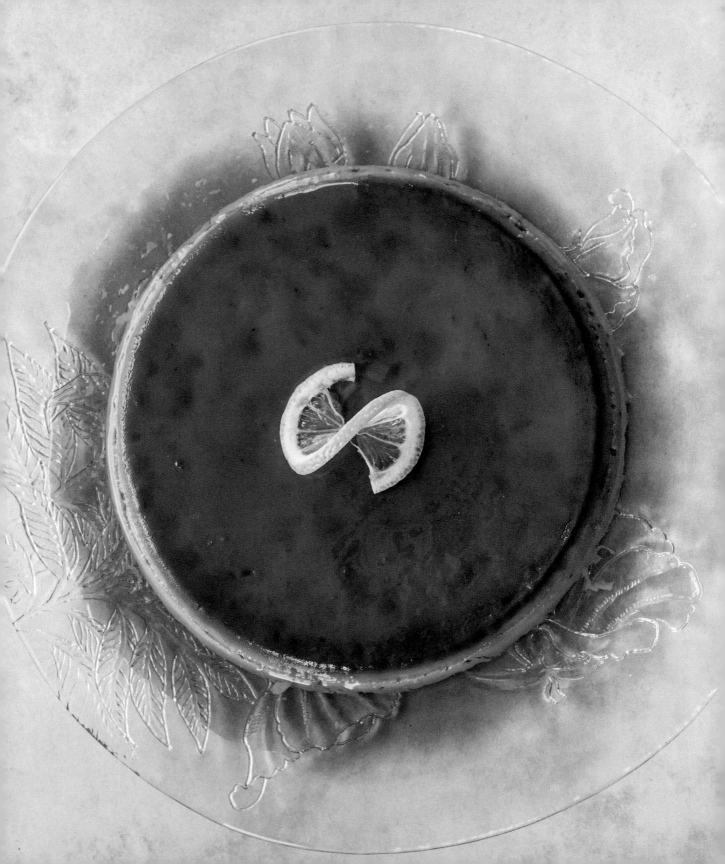

Now, on to the custard. Filipinos typically cook the custard using a traditional three-tiered pot and steam method. In this recipe, the custard will be baked. You will need a baking or roasting pan wide enough to fit the Pyrex nested in its center. In a large bowl, simply combine the egg yolks, condensed milk, evaporated milk, vanilla, and lemon juice with a fork. Yes, a fork, not a blender—we don't want air in this custard. Hold a sieve over the caramel-coated Pyrex and pour the egg mixture through it. Since we'll be baking, cover the Pyrex with aluminum foil and crimp along the rim for a nice seal. Now you're going to be performing a cool technique I learned—baking in a water bath. That's what the bigger roasting pan is for, to make a water bath. It's so very E-Z and helps the custard to cook evenly, resulting in a smooth and creamy flan.

Pour hot water around the Pyrex until it reaches about halfway up the sides. Place the nested pans in the oven, and bake for 50 minutes to 1 hour. Insert a toothpick or knife in the center of the flan to see if it's finished, and if it comes out clean, you're good to go.

Carefully remove the Pyrex from the roasting pan and let it cool, covered, for 30 minutes. Then remove the foil cover and replace it with an overturned serving platter. You are going to perform the old "Flip" trick. Are you ready for this? Hold the platter and Pyrex clamped together with thumbs underneath and fingers on top, as if you're holding a sandwich. Breathe deeply a few times and think happy thoughts. Holding on tightly, quickly flip the sandwiched platter and Pyrex AWAY from you, so you get the flan on the serving platter and not on you. It's kind of a yoga move, and you did it. Namaste!

Now remove the Pyrex from the flan. You might need to shimmy it with the end of a butter knife. Cover until you're ready to serve it up. FLANTASTIC!

FLIP TIP: To separate eggs, I just crack an egg in my super clean hand, separate my fingers slightly while holding on to the egg yolk, and allow the egg white to drain out of my hand. But feel free to use the old jiggle-juggle of the yolk between two shell halves if that works better for you. Whatever floats your yolk!

PIPPIE'S TASTY TASSIES
(MINI PECAN TARTS)

My oh my, this dessert is named after my cutie-patootie sous chef and niece, Pip. We make batches and batches of these tasty treats, sometimes 3 days in a row during the holidays. We just can't seem to keep them on a plate when there's company over, so we hit the mixer and get to baking.

Yields 2 dozen tarts

1 stick (114 g) unsalted butter, room temp	1 tbsp (15 ml) vanilla extract
1 (8-oz [227-g]) package cream cheese, room temp	⅛ tsp salt
1 cup (125 g) sifted all-purpose flour	1 tbsp (14 g) unsalted butter, melted
1 large egg	½ cup (55 g) pecans, chopped
¾ cup (165 g) packed light brown sugar	Pinch of cinnamon, optional

In a mixer, beat together the butter and cream cheese on medium speed, then gradually add the flour. Remove the dough and form it into a ball. Place it in a bowl, cover it with plastic wrap and let it chill for 1 hour.

Grab another bowl and combine the egg, brown sugar, vanilla, salt, and melted butter. Mix with a fork and set aside.

Prep the mini muffin pans by coating each cup with nonstick spray.

After the dough is chilled, it's time to roll it out into a sheet ¾ inch (2 cm) thick. First, use a little flour to coat the rolling pin and cutting board to avoid sticking. Then cut and divide the dough into 24 pieces. Roll each piece into a ball, and then flatten them into mini disks. This just makes it easier to form each into the muffin mold. The dough should cover the entire muffin cup, from the bottom to the top of the sides. I try to work quickly, so the heat from my hands doesn't start melting the nicely chilled dough.

Preheat your oven to 325°F (163°C).

After all the cups are formed, it's time to scoop in the pecans. I use about ½ teaspoon of finely chopped pecans in each. Follow the pecans up with the sugar mixture. I find it easiest to use a small creamer or gravy boat for pouring. You don't want to fill to the top of the rim; two-thirds full is perfect. Alrighty now, it's time to top off each cup with another ½ teaspoon of finely chopped pecans, and feel free to use a pinch of the optional cinnamon.

You're doing great! Place the muffin pan on the center rack of the oven and bake for approximately 20 to 22 minutes. Don't worry if they don't look very golden brown. They'll still cook a bit in the pan after you take them out of the oven.

Let the tassies cool for 5 minutes before transferring them from the hot pan onto the cooling rack. Once they're cooled, arrange them onto your fanciest serving dish or platter.

Hurry and grab one for yourself, these tasty treats tend to disappear fast!

⌒ CHUNKY MUNKS COOKIES ⌒
(TRIPLE CHOCOLATE)

I had to work hard to find a civilized way to get my chocolate fix. Why? Are you familiar with the Cookie Monster? We're very similar. Hence, this recipe. It was literally born from eating dozens and dozens of chocolaty cookies . . . for research purposes, of course.

Yields 2 dozen cookies

2 sticks (227 g) salted butter, room temp

½ cup (100 g) white granulated sugar

1 cup (220 g) packed light brown sugar

2½ cups (313 g) all-purpose flour, sifted

½ cup (45 g) oats

1 tsp baking soda

1 tsp salt

2 eggs

2 tsp (10 ml) vanilla extract

2 tbsp (30 ml) orange juice, freshly squeezed

1 cup (168 g) semi-sweet chocolate baking chips (I recommend Ghirardelli)

1 cup (168 g) milk chocolate chips (I recommend Ghirardelli)

½ cup (88 g) 60% cacao bittersweet chocolate chips (I recommend Ghirardelli)

In a standing mixer, cream together the butter, white sugar, and brown sugar at high speed for a couple of minutes.

While that's creaming, in a separate bowl combine the flour, oats, baking soda, and salt, and set aside for a sec.

Add the eggs, vanilla, and orange juice into the mixer. I prefer the freshly squeezed juice of an orange, but processed OJ is fine too. Mix on medium–low, or you'll have a mess on your hands. After a couple minutes, the dough should be fluffy and light.

On a lower mixing speed, add the bowl of dry ingredients and blend for a minute. Remove the bowl from the mixer and use a spatula to fold in the chocolate chips.

The dough is ready to be formed into balls. I use a ¼-cup (60-ml) ice cream scoop for uniformity. After the balls are formed, freeze them in a bowl for a good 30 minutes. When the dough is cold before baking, the cookies hold their shape a bit better.

When the freeze time hits the halfway mark, switch on the oven to preheat to 300°F (149°C).

Since the cookies get quite large as they bake, you'll need two baking sheets for a dozen cookies. Each ball bakes into a 4-inch (10-cm) diameter cookie. I have been gifted a couple of silicone baking sheet liners, so my cookies never stick. Please use parchment paper or greased aluminum foil as liners, you won't regret it.

Time to bake. Arrange six balls of cookie dough 4 inches (10 cm) apart on the baking pans. Do not flatten them. Place them on the center oven rack and bake for EXACTLY 23 minutes.

After 23 minutes, take the baking sheets out, and cool the cookies on the sheets for 30 to 40 minutes to allow them to set.

Grab a glass of milk and start dunking!

⟋ LEMON SHORTIES ⟍
(WITH SHORTBREAD CASHEW CRUST)

This is my take on a lemon square dessert I've made for the little ones in my family, but with Filipino mojo added to it. The cashews pay homage to a decadent, buttery Filipino dessert called *Sans Rival*, which means "without rival," because it's just so darn good!

Yields 20 squares

CRUST

⅓ cup (49 g) cashews, optional

2 sticks (227 g) unsalted butter, cubed

1½ cups (188 g) all-purpose flour

¼ tsp salt

¼ cup (32 g) cornstarch

1 tsp vanilla extract

1 tsp baking powder

FILLING

8 large eggs

2¾ cups (550 g) granulated sugar

½ cup (63 g) all-purpose flour

1 tsp baking powder

1 cup (240 ml) fresh lemon juice (approximately 3 lemons)

Lemon zest, optional

TOPPER

¼ cup (30 g) confectioner's sugar

Start by preheating the oven to 325°F (163°C).

Let's get the shortbread crust going, because it actually gets baked twice. My handy food processor is used to make this as E-Z as possible. If you have one, place the cashews in and pulse it a few times to get a fine chop. If you don't have one, do the best you can chopping by hand. Set the cashews aside in a bowl.

In the food processor, or if you don't have one use a hand mixer, cream the butter and gradually add in the flour, salt, cornstarch, vanilla extract, and baking powder.

A Pyrex glass baking dish is my go-to, but if you have a metal pan, you need to turn up the oven heat to 350°F (177°C) and add 20 minutes to the baking time. The glass takes a bit longer to heat up, but when it does it gets super hot, hence the shorter baking time. Use a spatula to help pour out the crust mixture and spread it evenly onto your baking dish. Place it in the fridge for 10 minutes to firm it up.

After the dough is chilled, bake for 15 minutes on the highest oven rack, until the crust turns light brown.

Here is our chance to make the filling. Give your food processor a quick rinse and dry, then combine the eggs, sugar, flour, baking powder, lemon juice, and lemon zest if you're using it. Yup, just dump everything in and then mix with a few quick pulses, or use a bowl and whisk.

Once the crust has become golden brown, pour the filling mix over the crust and put it back in the oven for another 35 minutes.

When you remove it from the oven, the filling should look like it firmed up and set. Now the hard part—leave it alone to cool for a ½ hour to make sure it's COMPLETELY cooled.

Once it's cooled, decorate with a good dusting of confectioner's sugar by using a fine mesh hand strainer or flour sifter. Cut into squares with a sharp knife. I like using a wee bit of nonstick spray on the blade to ensure a clean slice.

This will make a shortbread lover outta you!

～ UBEKINS ～
(UBE CHEESECAKES)

Kudos to my niece, Pip, for helping me develop this wonderfully smooth dessert as an homage to our Filipino roots—or, should I say, our yams. The star ingredient is *ube*, which is a bright purple yam with a nutty, vanilla taste. It's sweeter than a sweet potato, and commonly used in desserts. Recently, it's become more popular in the U.S. in many desserts and smoothies. Hopefully this trend won't end. By the way, it's also high in antioxidants, vitamins, and fiber!

Yields 12 mini cheesecakes
(6-oz [170-g] ramekins)

UBE

4 tbsp (56 g) unsalted butter

2 cups (480 ml) unsweetened coconut milk

1 (14-oz [414-ml]) can condensed milk

1 (12-oz [340-g]) jar ube jam (available in many online Asian stores or your local specialty market)

CRUST

1 cup (120 g) graham crackers, crumbed

¼ cup (56 g) unsalted butter, melted

FILLING

2 (8-oz [227-g]) packages cream cheese

¼ cup (56 g) unsalted butter, cubed

½ cup (100 g) white granulated sugar

1 tbsp (15 ml) fresh lemon juice

1 tsp vanilla extract

Dash of salt

¼ cup (60 ml) heavy whipping cream

TOPPERS

Graham crackers, crumbed

4 tbsp (60 ml) honey

½ cup (84 g) mini chocolate chips, optional

½ cup (50 g) crushed pistachios, optional

½ cup (50 g) coconut shavings, optional

For the ube, grab yourself a small pot, and melt the butter over a low heat. Add in the coconut milk, condensed milk and the ube jam to make your magic ube concoction. Combine well and be sure to keep an eye on it, no burning the yummy ube please. Cook for just 5 minutes, then take the pot off the heat. Transfer the mix to a bowl and refrigerate.

For the crust, place the graham cracker crumbs into a bowl. Drizzle with the melted butter and mix well. This should form a pliable consistency, much like wet sand.

Divide it into 12 (6-ounce [170-g]) ramekins and press to form a crust, making sure to build up the sides.

For the filling, beat and combine the cream cheese, butter, sugar, lemon juice, vanilla and salt. Set aside.

In a separate bowl, whip up the heavy whipping cream. It's easier to use a stand mixer on a medium setting than to do it by hand with a whisk. Use a cold mixing bowl to keep the cream at a cool temperature for E-Z whipping. It prevents the cream from melting and makes for a light, fluffy cream. Whip the cream for 7 to 8 minutes. Over whipping, beyond 8 minutes, will cause the cream to become too firm and grainy. The best stage of whipped cream is when it holds firmly but has slightly softened tips.

Add the whipped cream to the cream cheese mixture, and whisk until thoroughly combined.

You're in the final stretch. Take the cooled ube mixture out of the fridge, and gently fold it into the whipped cream mixture.

It's time to fill up the ramekins. Simply scoop up the mixture with a spoon, plop it into each ramekin, and smooth it out. It's best to fill each ramekin only three-quarters of the way up. Cover each ramekin with plastic wrap. Pop them into the freezer for 1½ hours to firm them up before serving.

Add some pizzazz by sprinkling crumbed graham crackers and drizzling a teaspoon of honey onto each ubekin. You can also add your own favorite toppers, or choose from the others I've suggested that taste terrific with it!

TITO'S CHOCOLATE CHIP PANCAKES

I know, I know, this isn't a dessert, but it IS a sweet breakfast goodie that I eat at any time of day. It was first made for me when I was a teenager, by my late uncle and godfather—in Flip talk, my Tito Carl. When he made pancakes for the family, he would artfully pour a stream of batter, which I call "drizzle-draw," into the pan in the form of each lucky recipient's first initial. He'd turn and say, "THIS is how to make them taste better," as he slid a bottle of Karo syrup my way. Yup, Karo.

Well, I have to agree, Tito—personalized pancakes always taste the best! I'm honored to say his tradition continues. Through the years, I've tweaked his recipe to satisfy my sweet tooth, and to make the pancakes a little lighter and fluffier. Shout out to my fellow Flips—it tastes like *puto*. For you non-Filipinos, that's a soft and fluffy sweet, steamed cake, one of my favorite desserts. Tito, I hope you approve of this version, and if you're watching, this one's for you. *Salamat Po*!

Yields 10 pancakes

1 large egg

2 cups (250 g) all-purpose flour

4 tsp (18 ml) baking powder

¼ tsp baking soda

⅓ cup (66 g) white granulated sugar

1 tbsp (15 ml) vanilla extract

4½ tbsp (63 g) unsalted butter, melted and cooled, divided

1 (12-oz [355-ml]) can evaporated milk

2½ tbsp (13 g) cocoa powder

¼ tsp salt

½ cup (84 g) semi-sweet chocolate chips

Whisk the egg first in a separate bowl to incorporate air into it, which will make a fluffier pancake. In a large bowl, combine the egg, flour, baking powder, baking soda, sugar, vanilla, 4 tablespoons (60 ml) of melted butter, evaporated milk, cocoa powder, and salt.

Grab yourself a griddle and warm it over a medium heat. I like using a flat griddle, but you can also use your favorite nonstick skillet. Melt the remaining ½ teaspoon of butter to lightly coat the surface. Scoop up about ½ cup (120 ml) of batter into a ladle and "drizzle-draw" the batter onto the hot butter. To test your creative skills, you'll have to draw the letter backwards, so that when it's flipped over it reads correctly. It's best to form a thick block letter to make it easier. No one's grading handwriting here. I've also made these pancakes using a squeeze bottle with a pointy tip, like those old-fashioned diner ketchup bottles. To do that you'll have to take out any lumps in the batter, or else the spout will clog.

Scoop up another ½ cup (120 ml) of batter and pour it over and around the letter that you just drew to form a regular circular pancake. Immediately sprinkle chocolate chips on top. I strategically place my chips to ensure a good chip-to-bite ratio.

After a couple of minutes you'll see a bunch of bubbles start to form throughout the batter, as well as a golden brown color along the edges of your pancake letter. OK, it's go time—"Flip" it over. Nice job! Now cook that side for another minute or two, the second side cooks quickly. Carefully slip the spatula under your creation and plate it up.

The remaining batter may start to thicken the longer it sits in the bowl. Loosen it up by adding a teaspoon at a time of water, as needed, and mix well. Continue cooking the rest of the batter, and remember to coat the griddle with melted butter before you make each pancake.

I hope you try personalizing a batch of chocolate chip pancakes for your family, and that you serve them up with a hug. Complement them with my Hello, Blueberry Compote! (page 168) or, of course, your tastiest maple syrup.

The Miscellaneous Zone

Here I've penned with good intention my final chapter, beyond that which I had planned. Creations that were passed along and tweaked, proven timeless as infinity. It is the middle ground of recipes from a simple dressing to a more complex sauce, between using precise measurements to adding just a pinch. It lies between the growls of hunger pains to the satisfaction of a stuffed belly. This, as you can imagine, will add new dimensions to your food. It is the chapter which I call . . . *The Miscellaneous Zone*.

(Hey, that was pretty good, right?!)

LUCKY DUCKY SAUCE
(SWEET 'N' SOUR)

This is my version of the typical duck sauce that you find in Chinese restaurants. If you made my *Quekiam* (page 10), woohoo, you did it! Please don't serve the pork 'n' shrimp egg rolls without this, you know why? 'Cause they're just TOO good together. You also need this tasty, tangy sauce to go along with any of these other recipes of mine: Tempting Tempura (page 84), Oh Boy, Po' Boy! (page 87), or even Veggie Rollee Polleez (page 35).

Yields 3¼ cups (760 ml)

3 tbsp (45 ml) veggie oil

Pinch of red pepper flakes, optional

½ cup (120 ml) ketchup

2½ cups (600 ml) chicken broth (swap with veggie broth if you prefer)

1 cup (200 g) white granulated sugar

½ cup (120 ml) white distilled vinegar

¼ cup (60 ml) sweet pickle juice, optional

Pinch of salt

2 tbsp (16 g) cornstarch

2 tbsp (30 ml) water

In a medium saucepan, heat up the oil and add the red pepper flakes for an optional bit of heat. Add the ketchup, and sauté for a minute or two on low-to-medium heat. Mix in the chicken broth, sugar, vinegar, pickle juice, if using, salt, cornstarch, and water. Bring to a light boil. Lower the heat and simmer for 5 to 10 minutes, until the sauce thickens.

You see, this was so simple! Get to dippin' ya lucky duck!

FLIP TIP: If you want a sweeter, chunkier sauce, add ¼ cup (41 g) of freshly chopped pineapple. If you lean towards a spicy kick, add 3 pepperoncinis and 3 to 4 tablespoons (45 to 60 ml) of pepperoncini juice to the sauce.

～ ONE-TWO PONZU ～
(CITRUSY SOY)

This is the über simplified version of the Japanese citrus-based ponzu sauce. The OG of ponzu sauce consists of: Lemon zest, lemon juice, soy sauce, edible kelp, dashi, a Japanese soup stock, rice wine vinegar and/or *mirin*, a Japanese cooking rice wine, or *sake*, an alcoholic Japanese beverage. Dang, that does sound good—but complicated!

I use this for tons of dishes: As a dipping sauce for sushi, like my Kinda Cali Rolls (page 81), or with fried foods like my Tempting Tempura (page 84), or as a marinade for meats and fish like my *Carne Asada* (page 66), or as a topper for my Fried Rice Frenzy (page 105). I also use ponzu as an E-Z dressing for noodles and sautéed veggies. You could buy store-bought ponzu, but this homemade version is so E-Z to make!

My basic combo of ingredients for ponzu sauce is the juice of one lemon mixed with ½ cup of soy sauce. That's all she wrote!

One-Two Ponzu.

Dip-dunk-done.

FLIP TIP: For fish and meat marinades, add fresh ginger and a vinegar of your choice. For fun party presentations, dress it up by adding chopped green onions. Pssst, I also love it with toasted sesame seeds. Here's a quick sesame seed to-do: In a dry pan, toast seeds on low heat for 2 minutes to release the oils and bring out that familiar sesame oil aroma. Then sprinkle some in!

Yields ¾ cup (180 ml)

4 tbsp (60 ml) fresh lemon juice	½ cup (120 ml) soy sauce

ASIAN PERSUASION DRESSING

This is gonna be a short one guys. I wanted to add a little Asian flair to a basic vinaigrette, so I concocted a recipe to satisfy my Filipino taste buds. This is not only the must-have dressing for my Beets an Everyday Salad (page 32), it's also the perfect change-up from that everyday dressing.

Mix all the ingredients together in a bottle or a mason jar and do a shimmy-shake. Drench your salad with this tangy, sweet, sesame-infused dressing. You'll want to put it on everything!

Yields 2 cups (475 ml)

1 tsp sugar

1 tsp sesame oil

1 tbsp (15 ml) fresh lemon juice

1 tbsp (15 ml) ketchup

1 clove garlic, minced

2 tbsp (30 ml) Dijon mustard

⅓ cup (80 ml) red wine vinegar

½ cup (120 ml) good quality olive oil

½ cup (120 ml) veggie oil

½ tsp salt

8 turns of freshly ground black pepper

⅓ cup (80 ml) water

~ FLIP DIP ~
(GARLIC VINEGAR)

I hope you love garlic. This dip is great with veggies, or try it over fried pork chops, it's delicious. In the Philippines, we call this dip *sukà*. Whatever you're eating, this complementary sauce is sure to be one you'll be making for years to come.

Yields ⅔ cup (160 ml) or 1 cup (240 ml) with veggie drippings added

⅔ cup (160 ml) distilled vinegar

5 cloves garlic, minced

½ tsp salt

¼ tsp freshly ground black pepper

⅓ cup (80 ml) veggie drippings from Veggie Rollee Polleez (page 35), optional

2 green onions, chopped

Add the vinegar, garlic, salt and pepper to a bowl. If you made my Veggie Rollee Polleez, whisk together the drained juices we saved from the cooked veggies. Also, just for looks, add the green onions to garnish. I find it easiest to eat this by spooning in the sauce, not dipping, otherwise you'll end up with veg all up in your sauce, and we don't want that.

Flip Dip—it's a quickie and a goodie!

~ FOOLS 'N' SAUCES ~
(2 COCKTAILS)

I grew up watching ridiculously funny and sometimes racy British comedies like *Benny Hill, Absolutely Fabulous*, and, as I got older, a bit of *Faulty Towers* and *Only Fools and Horses*. In honor of the latter, I've created two types of scrumptious cocktail sauces. One is a classic North American sauce with a twist, and the second is more of a traditional British prawn sauce, sometimes called a Marie Rose Sauce, that's a mayo-based sauce with a pale color and a kick of heat. Both of these sauces are great to serve with all types of fish and seafood, like my Lovely Jubbly Fish 'n' Chips (page 78) and Crabby Cakes (page 29).

For both sauces, simply combine the ingredients, mix well, and refrigerate until it's time for the shindig . . . or to watch something on the telly.

Yields 1 cup (240 ml) for each

COCKTAIL SAUCE WITH A TWIST	MARIE ROSE COCKTAIL SAUCE
1 cup (240 ml) ketchup	1 cup (240 ml) mayo
1 tbsp (15 ml) lemon zest, finely grated	2 tbsp (30 ml) ketchup (yup, the Brits snuck some in)
2 tbsp (30 ml) fresh lemon juice	2 tsp (10 ml) fresh lemon juice
2 tbsp (30 ml) prepared horseradish	1 tsp Worcestershire sauce
½ tsp Worcestershire sauce	½ tsp hot sauce, like Tabasco
½ tsp Sriracha, "The Twist," or Tabasco hot sauce	Pinch of salt
Pinch of salt	Pinch of cayenne pepper
1 tsp brown sugar, optional	

∼ CHEEZ LOEEZ! ∼

YAY, MY CHEESE RECIPE! I . . . LOVE . . . CHEESE! I always have, and I always will. To have and to hold, from this day forward . . .

Yields 2½ cups (620 g)

2 tbsp (28 g) unsalted butter

2 cloves garlic, minced

¼ tsp salt

⅛ tsp freshly ground black pepper

½ tsp cayenne pepper

3 cups (339 g) medium cheddar cheese, grated (grate the cheese yourself for a creamier sauce)

1 cup (240 ml) light cream

In a sauté pan over very low heat, melt the butter. Add the garlic, salt, black pepper, and cayenne pepper. Cook a minute, keeping an eye on the pan to make sure the garlic isn't burning. Mix and fold in the cheese, using a spatula, for 2 minutes. Slowly add the cream, and continue mixing and cooking over low heat until the sauce has an even consistency. This probably will take no more than 5 to 7 minutes.

Definitely serve with my Fresh Fries Please, I'll Wait! (page 41), or pour on WHATEVER!

AIOLI MOLI

The first time I heard of aioli, I thought both "Wow, that sounds yummy!" and "Oh, how fancy." I ended up loving this rich and creamy, emulsified sauce, and I told myself I would have it with every sandwich and crab cake thereafter. If you're not familiar with aioli, it's basically a mayonnaise-based mixture seasoned with garlic. Simple, yet loaded with flavor. It sounds more complex than it is.

Indulge me for a moment of food science. Aioli is an emulsion, which refers to two liquids that would normally not mix together, and are forced to mix, yet still maintain their distinct characteristics after being combined. In the case of hollandaise or aioli, the emulsification results in a creamy, fluffy sauce that really tops off a meal flavorfully.

This is not a standard aioli, where you would use raw eggs yolks and stream in olive oil as you whisk. I adapted it using a shortcut mayo base.

Yields 1 cup (240 ml)

1 cup (240 ml) mayo	3 cloves garlic, finely minced
2 tsp (10 ml) fresh lemon juice	Pinch of salt
1 tbsp (15 ml) olive oil	Pinch of pepper

Toss all the ingredients in a medium bowl and whisk vigorously for 5 minutes. The result will be a citrusy, garlic-flavored sauce that will look like mayo but have a creamier consistency. This makes sense, because technically aioli means mayo-like sauce.

If you ventured to make my Crabby Cakes (page 29) or my Oh Boy, Po' Boy! (page 87), you need this sauce!

LADY REMOULADE

I love remoulades, and when a recipe calls for one, I overdo it with this sauce. It's a terrific condiment for veggies, seafood and sandwiches. My remoulade is a mix of the classic French remoulade, which has hints of anchovy flavor and is why I use Worcestershire, and the creole Louisiana remoulade, which uses more herbs and spices like mustard and dill. Both pair well with seafood.

The Dijon will give this sauce a medium-yellow color, and it will have a similar taste to tartar, but spiced up. You end up with a subtle crunch from the dill pickle, a tanginess from the Worcestershire, and a mild, licorice/anise flavor from the French tarragon spice.

Using some elbow grease, combine all of the ingredients and mix well. I recommend refrigerating the sauce for a few hours prior to serving, as the longer you let it sit, the better the flavors meld.

Yields 1 cup (240 ml)

1 tbsp (15 ml) Worcestershire sauce

1 tbsp (15 ml) Dijon mustard

¼ tsp dried tarragon

1 tbsp (4 g) fresh parsley, chopped

2 tbsp (30 g) dill relish, not a sweet one

1 cup (240 ml) mayo

1 tsp fresh lemon juice

1 tbsp (15 ml) olive oil

3 cloves garlic, finely minced

Pinch of salt

Pinch of pepper

⌁ HELLO, BLUEBERRY COMPOTE! ⌁

If you're a 4 *Levels* fan, you'll remember me cooking this compote up in the waffles show. I think this is a must-make for waffles, pancakes, French toast, crepes, ice cream, cheesecake, pound cake . . . I could go on. This recipe works great with strawberries, raspberries, blackberries, and my new fave, gooseberries. I told you that I had the perfect complement to go with Tito's Chocolate Chip Pancakes (page 149)! Plus, it wouldn't be right if I didn't share this one with you . . . for old times' sake.

Heat a small saucepan over low heat, and add the blueberries, sugar, water, lemon juice, and salt. Bring to a boil for 5 minutes, then reduce heat and simmer for another 5 minutes, stirring occasionally. The compote should yield a watery consistency, just as my mouth waters every time I cook this up. As the fruit combines with the other ingredients, the berries will burst open and their juices will create a deep, blue-colored syrup.

HELLO, BLUEBERRY COMPOTE!

Yields 2 cups (640 g)

3 cups (444 g) fresh blueberries or 3 ½ cups (543 g) frozen

5 tbsp (75 g) white granulated sugar

4 tbsp (60 ml) water

3 tbsp (45 ml) fresh lemon juice

Pinch of salt

Mucho Thanks

It's been an honor and a privilege to share my cookbook with all of you folks. While compiling this collection of family recipes, I went on quite a journey. I had to hold on tight, twisting through the unexpected roller coaster of emotions. The process went from fun tapping into childhood memories, to the frustration of deciphering scribbles on scraps of paper found in a box. In the end, creating this array of dishes proved immensely gratifying, no matter how many gray hairs I have now. It's been the experience of a lifetime.

I would like to first give a BIG thank you to my sister, Kitty, my nieces Grace and Pip, and of course my brother-in-law, Simon—a.k.a. Team Burgess. Gracias for being my biggest food and writing critics, and for always keeping me humble and in check.

A big belly thanks to my brother Vinnie, for sharing his famous recipe, and hugs to my sister-in-law, Maryann, and nieces Casey and Allie. Also, a very special shoutout to my OG egg roll eaters and first nieces, Erica and Jamie.

Cheers to my brother Luke, you've earned The Top Taste-Tester Award. Thanks for always being the brave guinea pig for my new recipes, and for finishing every spoonful without complaint.

A heartfelt thank you to my Lolas, Titas, Titos and cousins, you are in EVERY MEMORY of my childhood, from fun to food. *Pinoy Power! Leche Flan*tastic (page 136) is dedicated to my aunt Tita Teresita Luarca Davis—your flan will be passed on for generations! Tito Carl's Chocolate Chip Pancakes (page 149) is dedicated to my uncle and godfather, Carlos Jesus Villanueva de Vera—your pancakes will be loved forever!

Thanks to all of my friends and family for unanimously electing me The Cook at EVERY party, and for surviving to eat another day. ;)

My sincerest thanks to everyone on the Page Street Publishing team for believing in me, and for believing that my cooking style would be of interest to the masses.

A GIGANTISAUROUS THANK YOU to Epicurious and *4 Levels* for giving me the platform to show the world how much I enjoy cooking.

And lastly, big hugs and kisses to Mom and Pop, my BIGGEST FANS. I'm truly grateful for your love and support, and especially for the fact that you decided to have that *one* last kid. This one's for you, folks!

All About Lo

Lorenzo is most recognized as a "Level 2 Home Chef" on the hit Epicurious YouTube series *4 Levels*. He became a fan favorite because of his fun play-by-play commentary that makes him hilarious to watch. He is known for his infectious laughs and his "big hug" personality, which makes you want to cook along with him.

He was featured in a 2019 interview with *Business Insider* titled "The Secret Sauce to YouTube's Viral Food Personalities." Lorenzo stated, "I never really thought I would be on a cooking show. In my mind, I just shake my head and think I'm just a guy who always cooked." He was described as possibly being the star of the series in regards to relatability, since "every video featuring him is loaded with comments about his 'dad' and 'uncle' energy, his enthusiasm, and how good his dishes end up looking." Plus, his videos consistently get millions of views.

Lorenzo is also a prolific actor. He admits he fell into this trade accidentally, after being asked to audition for a commercial because of his cooking knowledge. It was his childlike approach and good knife skills that helped him get cast as a chef in his first commercial in 2013. This gave him the confidence he needed to pursue acting full-time. Presently, he maneuvers between *4 Levels* and shooting ads for the likes of Vita Coco, *Charlie on Broadway,* and Google, to name a few—this list is long.

Although he likes working in NYC, he resides in the Hudson Valley and loves living an upstate life. He enjoys being able to play tennis with a mountain as his backdrop, and appreciates the simple pleasures of being outdoors, the best medicine in his book. He dreams of being able to travel the world someday, but not necessarily to see the sights. Instead, he looks forward to tasting every tapa the world has to offer. An undeniable foodie, that's Lorenzo. Find him on Instagram @rollinabenzo.

Index to Yumminess